C000134021

What an inspiring book, Duncan has a gift of maki... and laughing the next. S... umph over adversity and l... in place in our lives. Than... you, I can't recommend Get Over Indulgence highly enough.

LIZZY, WEST MIDLANDS, UNITED KINGDOM.

Duncan has a unique ability to take you on a riveting journey. You literally are transported into a world of intense emotions. It's like being on a rollercoaster but when it comes to an end, you are left with life lessons to ponder. If you haven't read this book, do yourself a favour, you will thank me later, it really will blow your mind.

SUZGO, CAPE TOWN, SOUTH AFRICA.

If you want to learn to jump out of bed and embrace the world, this is the book for you.

GLEN, NUNEATON, UNITED KINGDOM.

Get Over Indulgence is a light-hearted, engaging journey towards becoming a better human. It sucks you in – carrying you along with moments of mild surrealism, searing honesty, humour and joy – before delivering an unexpectedly powerful sucker punch. It will gently take you by the hand and show you the way forward. It is an engaging and accessible read, good for anyone thinking they'd like to take a step away from things that are holding them back and towards a brighter future. Oh and the soundtrack is great too.

KATHARINE, LONDON, UNITED KINGDOM.

This book has challenged me to stop making excuses. I never felt like I was someone with strong willpower, determination or focus. Get Over Indulgence presented a simple and effective way to overcome indulgence of any kind. Best of all it doesn't require will power, determination or focus. Thank you Duncan.

ANDY, SYDNEY, AUSTRALIA.

I found this book invaluable. When I started it I was really nervous, but by the time I'd finished I was chomping at the bit to get started on my new life. It is intelligent, captivating, motivating, inspiring, and fun. I'm truly grateful for the skills Get Over Indulgence has armed me with and can't recommend it highly enough!

HARLEY, NEWPORT, UNITED KINGDOM.

Duncan's story of personal transformation is second to none. It is authentic, captivating and very relatable. The steps that he teaches on how to overcome over-indulgence helps to simplify the complex struggle of recovery. Get Over

Indulgence is a brilliant book and I would recommend you get a copy, in fact, would you like to borrow mine?

BLESSAN, THIRUVANANTHAPURAM, INDIA.

"Getting Over Indulgence" is a deeply personal story of self-forgiveness and redemption. Duncan's superb memoir and scrutiny underscore the precept that, until we know what we want, it is expressly difficult to be ok with ourselves — no matter how much we achieve. Duncan has lived an unusually accomplished life that outwardly appears charmed; one for all intents and purposes of great achievement. This makes it all the more powerful to learn his story behind the story. This is an honest and stark appraisal, enlightening for those trying to understand and approach their own or others' lives of indulgence. The work is filled and enriched with disarming, enjoyable, and revealing self-deprecating humor.

JUDI, SANTA FE, USA

I have spent too much time watching videos on my phone to relax after long workdays at the hospital. Through Duncan's story of indulgence with alcohol and junk food, I have realised how my habit contributes to feeling more stressed at work and at home. This book has enabled me to name, confront, and overcome my indulgence.

TOM, BERN, SWITZERLAND

Duncan Bhaskaran Brown

Get Over Indulgence

Take Control
Find Your Stress-Free Life

Never forget, you are enough.

BhaskaranBrown.com

Abingdon 2022

A catalogue record for this book is available from the British Library

Cover design by Tanja Prokop
Interior design, formatting and type setting by Graciela Aničić
Back cover photograph by Martin Wackenier.

ISBN: 978-1-9999665-7-7 (paperback)
ISBN: 978-1-9999665-2-2 (audiobook)
ISBN: 978-1-9999665-0-8 (ebook)

First Edition: March 2022

10 9 8 7 6 5 4 3 2 1

For my Mother

It was a long journey, calling in at many dodgy
neighbourhoods, but with your help I got there.

You can learn how to PLAY the game.

JOHN LENNON

THE RUDDER JITTERS LIKE A HOODLUM PINNED BY ONE of Spiderman's webs. Captain Kertwang steadies the wheel. He wills his power into the skiff, urging it not to falter. The stakes are high. "Egads! They're close," shouts the squat first mate, solid despite the shaking engine and gargantuan swell.

The trawler seesaws on the chop as the sun cracks the horizon. The villainous crew lug corroded barrels onto deck. An enormous freebooter scans the surf – is that an engine? He ignores it and hoists a drum, preparing to dump the noxious cargo over the gunwales.

Sploosh! Captain Kertwang powers the boat over a crest. "Ahoy!" bellows the first mate as he sights the trawler. The captain spins the wheel. The boat arcs a wave into the air as it slows to engage.

The toxic-wasters panic. They scurry, striving to get their ship moving.

"Stop, by mandate of the United Nations!" The Captain's heroic voice booms from the loudhailer. His firm grip aims the harpoon while holding the wheel steady.

Kapow! The spear skewers the trawler's engine block.

"That's how you save the planet," says Captain Kertwang with a grin as bright as an admiral's buttons. The first mate nods.

The radio breaks in. "Duncan." The noble seafarer ignores it; he is going to incarcerate these marauding polluters. "Time to go, Duncan."

The eco-hero struggles but his control stick is just a chair leg. He strains but the bow is just a washing basket. He resists but the pirates are just toys. "Duncan, time for school".

The fantastical scene evaporates – dread kicks in. Captain Kertwang does not want to go to school, he wants to save the world. Psychotic enviro-terrorists he can handle; the other kids at school? That is an *entirely different matter.*

The school was filled with artwork that only a mother could love and children that even she was struggling with. The utilitarian cream corridor hummed with undergroomed, overstimulated fiendlings. I paused before the door. I could do this. Breathe.

As I shambled into the room I immediately attracted unwanted attention.

"Look, it's strangely Brown," shouts a bully.

Ignore them.

"Holy cow, it's crapman!" says another pest.

Let it slide.

"Don't they have full-sized clothes on your planet?"

Don't make eye contact.

"Your mum's fat"

And they call me stupid?

I made it to my desk with nothing more than shame scars. I did mention this to my mother. I knew wearing shorts to school was a bad idea, but she told me everybody wore shorts in the summer term. I appear to be the only one of everybody.

A shadow fell through the door with the weight of a guillotine's blade.

Fear filled the room. Bullies quivered. Tough kids whimpered. One boy dived for cover. Silence engulfed.

The aperture was filled with a diabolical slave-driver. I know that everyone is tall when you're a kid but I swear he must have been eight feet from top to talon. His hair was thinning, his eyes were like bullet-holes, his nose a beak curved like an orcish knife.

Mr Gannet, the man who is teaching us despair and impotence.

"Good morning class," he said in a misanthropic wheeze.

"Good morning Mr Gannet," we parroted.

"Today you are going to start new exercise books. You will use them to learn Roman history. Emma, hand them out."

Emma, a girl destined for the nunnery, passed around exercise books that are as vacant as our knowledge of Roman history. Mr Gannet issued convoluted instructions for the simple task of writing our names on the cover.

I successfully wrote my name. By successfully I mean that more ink went on the book than on my fingers.

Suddenly Mr Gannet flapped behind me. "What have you done!" I really couldn't see a problem. I'd done what he asked. I'd even go as far as to say that my handwriting was good – you could read it and everything.

"What have you done!" he screeched.

"I wrote my name on…." I tried to respond.

"But it's upside down."

"No, I wrote it the right way up."

"Don't take that tone with me, boy. The exercise book is the wrong way up."

"But the pages still work." I added with an uncertain smile.

Mr Gannet trained his iron-heated stare upon me. He did not blink because he had no eyelids. The rest of the class pretended to work while sneakily eyeing the unfolding drama.

"Boys and girls. Will you all show Duncan how an exercise book is supposed to look."

The children dutifully held up their books.

"Look at everyone else's books. Do you see the difference?"

I shook my head.

"Emma, explain to Duncan how an exercise book works."

Emma rose with a prim grace. She picked up her book with care, printed on the front in florid script was her name.

"Exercise books open from the left. If they open from the right you have it the wrong way around." she said with the enthusiasm of a collaborator.

"Everyone else's books go one way and yours goes the other," Mr Gannet said.

"Making it easy to find my book among all the others?" I said hopefully.

"Making you different, and that is your problem. You're a pig."

He said this as if it was the most profound statement I was ever likely to hear. Presumably my confusion led him to conclude that I had failed to understand this philosophical utterance.

"Look around you boy, this classroom is full of chickens and you are a pig. You're a pig in a chicken coop. Do you see, everyone, a little piggie is stuck in the coop," he said with obvious glee.

The children laughed.

"There's no place for pigs here. There's no place for difference here. There's no place for you in this classroom, no place in this world. There is *nowhere you can be* a pig."

Time stood still. He fixed me with his two orbs of eternal darkness; I held his totalitarian stare.

"But pigs are more intelligent than chickens." I said in a half whisper.

The class collectively drew breath. Every eye in the room was on me, in eager anticipation of what was about to happen.

Mr Gannet's beak flared in an exhalation of fury.

"See me after school."

A thousand fights, football matches and frantic kiss-chases whirled around me. I did not notice. I was slumped in the corner of the playground.

This was bad. This was very bad. My mum was going to kill me. I was in trouble with Mr Gannet, again. This was so serious it was probably going to cost me that Action Man that I've been after for ages. This was not good at all.

"Nowhere you can be…"

It kept sloshing around my head like an off-kilter washing machine. There must be somewhere I can be who I'm supposed to be, even if I was supposed to be a pig. I can't fail to fit into the whole world, can I? Is it only in the unreal world that I can be the real me? Is that the only place where I can be who I want to be?

"Nowhere you can be…"

A movement caught my eye and broke the spell. The new boy was waving. He was beckoning me to follow him. Before I could ask him what he wanted he was off.

This presented me with a problem: should I follow him? I didn't know him, yet there was something about him. I couldn't put my finger on it but he looked – familiar. And he was the only other person within half a mile that was wearing shorts.

I chased.

Across the playground, past the swings, over the field we went. Just as I was starting to catch him he darted through a hole in the fence. I plunged through. This, it turned out, was a mistake. On the other side was a steep drop.

Everything seemed to slow. I had time to look around. I could have reached out to pick a flower from the passing foliage. I even had time to wonder what was going to happen next. How deep was this abyss?

The landing, while not graceful, was not grievous. I decided to remain crumpled for a moment or two, just while I got my bearings.

"'Ello?" said the boy with a face that was as upside down as it was unkempt.

"Why are you the wrong way up?" I asked.

"Man, that's a pretty silly thing to say when you're lying in the dirt, in a heap," he said while helping me up.

We were in a bower, shot through with mystical sunlight. It seemed far, far away. Mr Gannet and the school seemed a long way off.

"You're right about pigs," he said.

"I am?" I replied.

"Yeah, pigs are better than chickens."

"They are?"

"Chickens are stupid, the best thing you can be is a pig."

"It is?"

"I'm Hank."

"I'm Duncan."

"Do you want to share my chocolate?"

Hank pulled from his pocket a battered but undefeated bar of Dairy Milk. I didn't mind that he broke off a square with his mud-streaked hands. I didn't mind that we had to sit in the dust. I didn't mind that the school bell would ring again and we would have to face the privations of Mr Gannet's school room.

A single streak of sunlight caught my block of chocolate. Illuminated, it seemed loaded with mythic significance. I delicately settled the morsel into my gob.

As the chocolate softened I disintegrated into gratification. I was surf-tossed into bliss. I was overcome with contentment. I had the strangest feeling that Hank and I now shared some secret bond; comrades, maybe? More like brothers? Twins?

I felt something new, something I thought I could only ever experience in my imaginary life, in my games. But here I was, in the world of hard packed mud and demonic teachers, feeling like I had just beaten back a horde of toxic waste dumping felons. I felt like Captain Kertwang, the swashbuckling eco-defender.

Merriment. I had a new friend. He'd brought solidarity to my life but more than that he'd brought the release of chocolate, the blissful surrender.

I walked back into the classroom with renewed confidence. I was a different person. I learnt something important about the ways of the world. I'd learnt to handle my problem just like the adults. But most important of all, I'd found my tribe. Sure, it was small, but it was *my* tribe – my drove of pigs.

I sat at my desk certain that I wasn't going to be like all those other suckers. I was different. I wasn't a mindless clucking chicken, I was a noble and imperious pig. I grinned. It was time to think my own thoughts, to walk my own path. No longer would I conform.

"Open your books and write Roman History at the top of the first page." Mr Gannet ordered.

He locked me in his steely gaze.

"And Duncan," he bellowed, "do it neatly."

OK, maybe I'd conform – temporarily.

I need
EXCITEMENT,
oh, I need it **bad**.

JOHN O'NEILL

THE WAREHOUSE WAS EMPTY SAVE FOR THE NAMELESS and formless throng that writhed to the untamed melody. I was just a microscopic cog in the catastrophic machinery of party.

God, was I afraid.

This was supposed to be the big one. This was supposed to be the party of the year – heck, this was supposed to be the party of my life. We weren't talking about jelly and ice cream. Hank and I had moved on from the Dairy Milk days. We had work boots, torn jeans and elegantly flopped haircuts that wouldn't look out of place on the zeitgeist.

We'd spent weeks preparing: planning which mademoiselle would get our attention, polishing the gems of chat up lines, agonising over which t-shirt to wear. I had it sorted, I was ready. I'd even had a shower.

But now there was a problem and it was slamming into my head harder than the feral backbeat.

"Hank, what am I going to do?" I said.

"Dude, it's just a warehouse party," he replied.

"Yeah… but what if they realise that I'm just a little kid pretending to be grown up?"

"Man, it's time to let you into a little secret,"

"What? Everyone else feels like a fraud?"

"No," Hank chuckled, "lager!"

"Lager?"

"Yeah man, have a couple of tinnies and relax," he said as he handed me a can of beer.

Tsst.

I took a swig. It was not to my taste. Warm. Bitter. Far too fizzy. Why does everyone go on about this stuff? It's foul. Of course I was too cool to spit it out, or even to stop drinking it. I mean everyone from my parents to my friends to the government make a big fuss about it but I wasn't feeling it. Nothing happened.

I finished the can for appearances sake. As it had no effect I took the second one that was offered. And the third. I was still feeling out of place, no point in making it worse by saying no.

Then it hit me. I understood what Hank was talking about. A comforting brilliance started to rise from my toes. Soon it had engulfed my whole body. I felt good. I felt confident. I felt alive. I could see the music. The beat pulsated at the rhythm of my over excited heart.

I moved through the crowd in a Brit Pop swagger. I strode on Cool Britannia. I resounded zig-a-zig-ah. I nodded at the blokes, smiled at the babes. I made Liam Gallagher look coy.

I broke onto the dance floor and began to strut the light fantastic. I flaunted it all to the slam of the ample sound system. Then the strains of Hey Jealousy by the Gin Blossoms drifted towards me with frenetic uncertainty. The floor began to clear but I was grinning. At last an unsung song, an unheralded melody – my chance to show off my grasp of the esoteric.

That's when I saw her. Her hair was golden, like ripe wheat. Her eyes were blue, like the azure sea. Her lips were red, like a pack of Marlboro. My muse in Doc Martens.

I danced up to her and we locked eyes. "You like the Gin Blossoms?"

"Yeah," she replied with studied nonchalance.

"That's cool."

"Yeah."

"Do you want to go for a walk? I've got lager."

"Yeah."

I put my arm around her and we sauntered to the door. There was Hank, watching like a Victorian cotton magnate watches a shipment heading to London. He grinned and stuck up his thumbs idiotically.

Success.

I never saw her again. In fact, I never even got her name. But that didn't matter, because when it's the first time, once is enough. Well, not with alcohol. With alcohol once was never enough. Hank and I embarked on many wild adventures throughout that summer daze.

But it couldn't last forever and soon the really real world clomped over the horizon.

I was a confident guy who would happily squeeze into any situation. Yet for some reason I couldn't get my head around the grown-up thing. I mean, I wasn't the kind of person who sought piles of cash, flash cars and vacant-minded, hard-bottomed chorus girls. I didn't need to pretend to be a big shot.

No, I was totally focused on making the world a better place. I was happy to do my bit to create utopia. I just needed to figure out a bit that was suitable for a man of my ability.

So I lived with Hank and developed a taste for red wine, blue cheese and green issues. I was happy to bang out my philosophy of environmental impacts to anyone who'd listen. That was mostly Hank though.

The low ceiling and rough-hewn walls made the place feel more like a cavern than a tavern. The kaleidoscope sparkle of the fruit machine flashed like a Christmas tree at Easter. I was out of place too. This evening I was not drinking. After bumming about in pubs for a while it dawned on me that I could earn some money on the other side of the taps; at the very least I'd be spending less.

So I became versed in the ways of the barkeep. I discovered that people talk to the bar – happy people, pleasant people, drunk people, crazy people. They weren't talking to me, they were having a therapy session with a slab of wood. Only occasionally would I get dragged in.

I was doing a good job of letting the wood do the talking until a dazzling woman flowed into the place like an art deco ballet dancer stepping out of a green Bugatti. She ordered and began a heated discussion with the bar top. I busied myself fixing her drinks but her discourse quickly turned environmental. She was stepping on one of my pet corns and I could not remain silent.

"Forget polar bears, no one cares about polar bears," I said.

"But Ursus Maritimus is at the heart of this egregious problem," she shot back like a floral missile.

"You have to relate it to things people can see. You have to talk about the air pollution on the road they walk down. Forget polar bears, no one cares about polar bears because there are no polar bears on our street – too remote."

"That's a well-considered position that would no doubt play well with the populous general."

"Thank you."

"I'm Kath," she smiled, "have you ever thought about getting involved in politics?"

The paint peeled from a once red door. The innocent letter box cunningly hid a vicious draft excluder. Shove leaflet, hope.

I was a politician. This was politician's work. It had happened innocently enough – I meet an interesting woman in a dull pub and my life had changed. Now I was standing for the epicenter of political power, Abingdon Town Council, and I had the leaflets to prove it.

In my imagination campaigning was about spending time at a printing press worn by bundled mountains of handbills. It was work to be done at midnight, almost certainly whilst evading the secret police.

In practice it involved a lot of front doors. If I wasn't pushing pamphlets through them I was knocking on them asking for support. You'd be surprised at the number of people who don't have doorbells. It's almost as if they don't want local politicians to pop by and say hello.

Blue door, nice knocker, next leaflet.

It was murky, it was dark, it was doleful. Yet something prevented me from seeking solace within the building.

Like the ancient Anglo-Saxon proverb says: "If I go there will be trouble. If I stay it will be double." I stared at my Rubicon rendered in steel and glass and breathed deeply; should I cross?

"Dude, it's only a leisure centre," said Hank.

Still I hesitated.

"It's not like we're going to the gym or anything," he added.

I walked through the door.

The count was an intriguing prospect. I'd only ever seen them on late night general election coverage and, frankly, I was curious. I had arrived good and early; I wanted courtside seats.

As I walked in I was confronted by a shrimp who was masquerading as an election official.

"You are here for the count, I presume." he said.

"Oh yes," I replied, affecting what I hoped was an air of eminence.

"In which case, you're late. Follow me." He sped off.

"You will be sitting here," he said and pointed at some chairs. I wanted to get close to the action but this looked too close.

"You will take one of these strips, you will place the votes on the strip. They will be straight on the strip or…"

"I hate to break it to you, but I'm not here to count the votes."

"Then whatever are you here for?"

"I'm one of the candidates."

"Really? You don't look old enough?" He sensed a trick.

"I moisturise," I replied and added my best grin.

"In that case you will go and stand in that corner and you will stop interfering with the electoral process." He trotted off leaving a wake of acrimony. I sauntered over to Kath.

"Are we verging on overwrought?" she asked.

"Not at all," I lied.

"You know there are three types of people here?"

"Really."

"Yes, there are those who must attend to the prosaic business of counting and those for whom mathematical acumen is not a forte."

I groaned. She pointed at this, explained that, nudged me in directions and showed me what to watch out for. I saw my votes piling up. This evening was going to flow like fine, vintage wine.

After several hours of tedium I accepted that there is only so much fun to be had watching people count slips of paper. Eventually the results started to slouch in. It was like a raffle without prizes – no one got a box of Roses or scented candles or anything. When they eventually got round to announcing that I had been elected it felt like an anticlimax. Sure, there were congratulations but there was no presentation. I didn't get a medal. I didn't get to stand on a podium. They didn't play my anthem, which is a shame as some Daft Punk would have livened things up.

But it didn't matter what the vibe in the place was because I knew it was a big thing. Here was something to sink my teeth into. This was something to aim my not inconsiderable talents at. I was not a narcissist – I was never seduced by the vainglory that took many people off to the city to become big shots. I rejected all of that. However, being a councillor would give me real power and authority. Of course, I only craved it for the good I could do with it.

After all, someone has got to deal with the climate emergency.

I plummeted onto the sofa, pleased but not elated. It had been an intriguing evening but it was far from a jig of buffoonery. How to enliven the affair?

"Well done dude, let's have a drink to celebrate," said Hank as he offered me a bottle of wine.

"I think I will," I replied.

"Would sir like some TV with that?"

"No, I think this calls for something harder."

"Party?"

"Paaaaarty!"

"Who should we invite?"

"Everyone on earth."

"We could do but we'd have to planet."

I made a few calls.

Franz Ferdinand tramped out their particular brand of post-punk revival at a volume that was just south of unacceptable. The lights were getting lower as we were getting higher.

I was trying to concentrate on the construction of a splendid and substantial joint when Steve crashed onto the sofa, imperiling the entire architectural endeavor. He hid his lamb's heart with a crocodile's smile.

"How do I address you, now you're a big cheese?" he asked.

"I'm pretty sure Duncan still works."

"OK your Duncan-ness, what are you going to do with all the money from all the bribes?"

I laughed. "Fine, it's Councillor Brown and I'm not going to get bribed."

"Will you get invited to one of those jollies that involve expensive meals and cheap hookers?"

I shook my head.

"Well, if you do, remember your old buddy Steve."

"You're going to make sure that I don't get wrapped up in my own sense of self-importance aren't you?"

"Your feet: kept on this ground. All part of the service."

I exhaled a billowing nebula of smoke and handed the joint to him.

"Nice work, Councillor Brown."

In the background Hank nodded.

She comes in COLOURS everywhere.

MICK JAGGER & KEITH RICHARDS

THE PURPLE SHIRT DOZED ON THE HANGER UNTIL I yanked it from the wardrobe. The fact that it was hung up was a strong indication that it might be clean. It was not my favourite but it was free from the sundry stains and smells that life leaves on clothing.

I only had part of my mind on dressing. A significant chunk rested on the future. I'd got myself elected – which was great – but what now?

"Looking good buddy," Hank said.

"Thanks, but what am I going to do with my new platform?" I asked.

He thought for a second. "You're always banging on about changing the world. Why don't you do that?"

"Can you change the world on a local council?"

"Don't know. Let's have a glass of wine before we go,"

"Hank, this is important,"

"Come on, it'll take the edge off."

We spent a lot of time taking the edge off. I was never entirely clear which edge I was trying to take off but something needed smoothing. Maybe I'd been a carpenter in a former life; I liked sunshine, cider and rustic barns so why not working the wood? Maybe that was why I had such a desire to scrape at the rough bits. Planing and sanding was obviously a consequence of my previous incarnation as a horny-handed son of toil.

"Cheers," I raised my glass.

"If you can't change the world," Hank smiled, "at least remember to change your pants."

A bright white ceiling embellished with bosses and coats of arms; it whispered elegance in carefully annunciated tones. The buffet was resplendent. Even attired in the fanciful robes of my elected office I felt out of place, underendowed.

Over the years I had learnt that the real business of any organisation is not conducted at its meeting but over drinks, usually after the meeting, though sometimes before. It was high time I settled into the real business.

"Look at the cheeeeese," said Hank.

"It is a lovely spread," I agreed.

"Mmm buffet."

I found some forgettable wine and a spot in the room that gave access to the buffet without looking desperate. The cheese was incomparable, the kind of stuff that makes your teeth tingle.

My attempt at civilised gorging was punctuated by the arrival of the Leader of the Council, a fairy godmother who had been retrained by the parachute regiment.

"Glad that's over for another year," she said in a mild yell.

Every fibre of my body wanted to shout "Sir, yes, sir," but I think I went with "indeed".

"It's time to have a stab at governing."

"That's not a…"

"You're young and young people are interested in all that climate stuff."

"As it happens I…"

"Good, I need a chair for the climate scrutiny committee."

"I'd be delighted but…"

"Good, I'll get the town clerk to send you the papers."

"One thing," I said quickly, somehow tricking her into listening.

"What?"

"Could we change the name to the environmental impacts committee because…"

"Call it what you like, just look busy and keep the lunatic fringe off my back."

She swept off, presumably to pressgang other unsuspecting councillors into the service of her greater good.

"She's done aggression training with a serial killer," Hank said.

"Yeah? How much did she charge him?"

I was engulfed in a wooden chair which was almost worthy of the title throne. It headed a huge table almost worthy of the title gargantuan. I was keyed up like a bordello piano.

"I'd like to call to order the first meeting of the Environmental Impacts Committee." Despite the nerves I managed to say it with a hint of pomposity. I looked around the table. In my mind this was going to be my team, in the next year we were going to achieve great things – possibly even reversing global warming.

In my mind I was Hannibal – not the Carthaginian general but top dog of the A-Team. As I studied the other councillors I realised I was in a room full of Howling Mad Murdocks. I chewed my imaginary cigar – how do I knock up a tank from this warehouse of cabbages?

"Why do I keep getting envelopes stuffed full of council papers through my door?" I asked, I always thought it was good to open with a question. The councillors looked stunned but the clerk, who disguised his undercurrents of Reading gaoler as organisational ability, was itching to answer.

"Under the 1974 Local Government Act the council has a legal responsibility to provide every councillor with every council paper. It's an oversight issue," he pointed out like he was stating something that would be self-evident even to a baby chicken.

"Have you heard of email?" I asked.

"Well obviously," his collected exterior showed the faint trace of a ruffle.

"It strikes me that we could save an area the size of the New Forest every year if we just sent more papers by email. Obviously, councillors would still need some papers, but even so, we're still talking about a substantial copse."

"I am minded to think we could perhaps look into it."

"How much do we spend each year on printing and postage?"

"We spend approximately £8,436 on committee printing and £3,762 on postage." He tried to say it casually but there was no hiding his encyclopedic delight.

"Great, we've just saved about ten grand." I grinned.

The clerk looked at me. He had assumed I was dinner and now it was dawning on him that I was the shark.

With that my reputation was cemented. All of the councillors that didn't care about trees liked the money we'd saved: all of the councillors who didn't care about money liked the trees we'd saved. Instant popularity.

Squelch, squelch, squelch. I mashed the turnip the way I had on a thousand other Sundays. In my family things didn't change; my parents had become fixed the way ivy becomes inseparable from walls. My mother was forming up battalions of potatoes and companies of carrots, as normal. My father was busied with some irrelevance that would guarantee he would be late to dinner, as normal.

Yet this Sunday was different – there was another place set at the table.

When my mother retired from her job she had to train the person that would replace her. Just after the appointment was made my mother started to go on about how beautiful her replacement was. I didn't give it much heed as I have questions about my mother's taste in women.

The doorbell rang.

"Go and get it then," said mother, "it'll be Sreeja".

I swear she was smirking, as if this obvious ruse of sending me to the door was a stroke of subtlety.

"Hello," said Sreeja.

"Errrm…" I sort of said.

I was shocked.

"Am I in the right place?"

"Errrm... Yeah... Errrm... Come in."

She smiled. There was an undercurrent of concern in the look. She'd spent the last few weeks with my mother and was probably expecting me to have it a little more together. I was not what she was expecting.

She was not what I was expecting. She was hot. Her family were from India and she managed to wear the bohemian, ethnic look very well. She had a cracking set of boots.

The room smelt age-old, like it had entertained the town's mayors for as long as there had been mayors. One or two of the councillors looked like they might have been around for the opening.

"The way he leapt to his feet to dispute the point was simply mercurial," said a set of haunted bagpipes trying to pass itself off as a councillor.

"Uhh," I replied.

I enjoyed socialising after meetings. It was a chance to fill your hand with a glass of wine and dissect the motions and commotions of the meeting. There were councillors who said far more after meetings than they ever did in them. In fact, some of them wouldn't shut up about it.

"It's your turn to be mayor, isn't it?" said the leader of the council as she ambushed me from behind an incidental plant pot.

"I believe so," I said with escalating fear.

It may sound strange to the untrained ear to say it's someone's turn to be mayor, but it is logical. The council operated an order of succession which meant that the most experienced councillor that had not been mayor would take the office for the next year.

"You are going to accept," she stated.

"I was thinking of passing, it's not really my sort of thing," I replied.

"It's not anyone's sort of thing but a young chap like you would give the council a powerful new image. You could do a lot to engage young people in the political process."

"I'm not sure I'd be good at it."

"Nonsense. We need you front and centre."

I wasn't sure what to say and before I had a chance to think of something…

"Good it's decided, you'll take over next month."

And that was that.

Oh heck. I hurriedly searched for Kath, desperately hoping that she could offer me some solace.

"What do mayors do?" I asked when I found her.

"They're like Tesco's," she said.

"Really?"

"Yes, every town has one and they're filled with food and drink."

The light streamed onto our table as if the sun had been placed in the heavens simply to light her path to me. I am not a follower of Zeus but when he sent this celestial being my way he was on a roll.

"What? 'The' Bruce Springsteen?" I asked with incredulity.

"Yes," said Sreeja.

"The Boss?"

"You don't approve?"

"No, far from it, I love Springsteen. I'm just surprised."

"Why?"

"It doesn't really fit with the whole yoga thing. Shouldn't you be listening to whale music?"

"I am capable of liking more than one thing, I'm a person not a caricature."

"I suppose it explains why you like dancing in the dark."

For a second her soulful expression was broken by a look that was frankly smutty.

If only it was that simple.

Unfortunately, she wasn't really my type. She didn't drink much. She didn't smoke. She didn't take drugs. She even ate chickpeas – strange. Despite that our first few dates had gone well and we were getting close. That wasn't the issue.

No, the problem was altogether more subtle. Normally, relationships develop at their own pace, outside the glare of public attention. They have the breadth and space to develop in the direction that they need to, unencumbered by constraint and obligation. But I had a dilemma. I had to pop the question right now. So I screwed my courage up into a ball.

"Do you want to be my mayoress?" I said as casually as I could.

"Your what?" She nearly spat out her scone.

"When I'm mayor, I'll need a mayoress."

"What do I have to do?"

"I'm not sure, probably just look pretty."

Scepticism crossed her face.

"It's a job you are more than adequately qualified to do." I quickly added with a covering grin.

"I'll do it, but I'm not going to do all the driving. If there's the chance of champagne we're taking your car."

"It's a deal."

The rest of the people in the cafe seemed oblivious; they continued to bustle around, carrying on with their lives. But for me the world stopped, for that perfect moment I was on top of it. I was about to reach the political heights, but better than that, a goddess had stepped out of the clouds to share it with me.

Yet there was doubt lodged somewhere at the back of my mind. What would Hank think? I know he wanted to come to events – the buffets, the free bars were all grist to his mill. How was he going to take it? Was he going to start getting jealous of Sreeja?

Then another question dropped by – was she going to get jealous of Hank?

"This year I'm going to party hard," I said bombastically.

Several hundred people drew breath. This was not what they were expecting from their newly elected mayor.

"Celebrating is what being mayor is all about. I want us to celebrate the achievement of every young person in this town. I want us to celebrate the accomplishments of every voluntary organisation in this town. I want us to celebrate the success of every business in this town. I want to celebrate with each and every one of you. Let's throw the party that this town deserves."

Euphoric applause. I took it. I had got the year off to a sensational start. It was going to be an out-and-out, grand slam triumph. It was going to be one Hank of a year.

With reverent care I removed the mayoral chain from its case. It was reassuringly heavy, smugly Victorian and worth more than my flat. For a moment I thought of all the people who had worn it before. Tonight was just a tiny crumb of a historic cake; but it was my crumb, my contribution.

You may wonder what mayors actually do all day. It's a fair question. As it lacked a job description there were times when I wasn't sure what I was doing. Occasionally I'd ended up in situations I had no idea how to deal with. I went to one event where I had to judge a fancy dress contest in a room full of people who weren't wearing fancy dress.

But I figure the most useful thing they can do is to spread joy. This may not seem like much but there is a potential in that gold chain. A small thing for me often meant a big deal to other people. I discovered I could make people's day simply by turning up, I could make them smile simply by talking to them. I quickly realised that this was my kind of power.

I got invited to many events. Mostly they were in Abingdon and as I grew up in the town I had very little trouble finding them. Tonight it was a celebration at the community centre on Blacknal Way.

"Glass of wine?" asked Hank.

"No, I'll be alright," I replied.

"Come on man, a little drink rocks the party."

"Maybe…"

"And you've already had a long day, you deserve it."

"Cheers."

Blacknal Way was only a brisk walk from the flat. I was warmed by the wine and the night was mild. I enjoyed the stroll. I used the time to think through some of the things that were looming. I had several big events to arrange and don't even talk about Christmas.

I rounded the corner and there was the community centre. It looked surprisingly dark for somewhere hosting a hoedown. And, now you come to mention it, the car park was empty too. I don't take myself too seriously and despite the occasional lapse into egotism I hope no one would accuse me of being pompous. It never bothered me if there was no one at an event to meet me, I'm a big boy. But I do insist that someone turns up and unlocks the building first.

OK, maybe I've got the wrong door. I wandered round the building, checking if there was another entrance. There wasn't.

OK, maybe I'm early. I hung around for a while but no one showed up.

OK, maybe I'm at the wrong place. It's possible, I didn't know that part of town well. I had a look around. I couldn't see another community centre.

"Excuse me, is there a community centre round here?" I asked a doddering dog walker.

"Yes, it's just over there," he replied with warmth.

"Oh, I've tried that one, is there another?" He looked bemused. I swear he wanted to ask if that one was not to my liking?

"I don't think so," he said as he shuffled away.

OK, maybe he's new to town and doesn't know the area...

After I'd ransacked the neighbourhood I decided that the event must have been canceled at the last minute and they hadn't been able to get a message to me. So I went home. Unhappily.

I unlocked the door and dragged myself and my dejection through it.

"Hey buddy, how was the event?" Hank said.

"I don't know, I never found it," I answered testily.

"What happened?"

"I don't know."

"Never mind, have a glass of wine, it'll cheer you up."

The glass had started to calm me down. I began to feel better and to think about what I could do with the rest of the uninhabited evening, but I kept returning to that empty community centre.

"It wasn't your fault, you tried," Hank said.

"I screwed it up, Hank. I'm missing something?"

"You did your best, have a top-up and maybe some cheese to take your mind off it."

"The invite!" It struck me like a thump from Thor's own hammer. It's in a folder!

I tore around the flat till I found it. I'd got the date – right. I'd got the time – right. I'd got the community centre...

"Oh."

"What's the matter?"

"It's the community centre on Blacklands Way."

"That's where you went?"

"No, I went to the community centre on Blacknal Way."

"Oh."

It was after nine – too late to go now. I'd screwed up and no amount of apologising was going to make up for that. I hadn't just dropped the ball, I'd fallen awkwardly onto it and burst it too. I felt like a scruffy boy who had been shouted at for writing in his exercise books the wrong way up. I was Mayor of Fraudsville.

Turn
and FACE
the **strange**.

DAVID BOWIE

I HIT SEND. THE MESSAGE DISAPPEARED AND WITH IT the exact amount of tension required to bend a steel beam. The last thank you dispatched, another e-mountain scaled. I leaned back. I'd schlepped my way through a protracted 18-hour day, yet every minute had held something to revel in.

Being an Abingdon lad, many events held my head up a little higher. Lots of pride: pride for the achievements of our people, pride for the opportunities offered by our groups, pride for our town.

While not technically in Abingdon, the council had developed a great relationship with Dalton Barracks, home to part of the Royal Logistics Corp. The station itself is a few minutes beyond the boundaries but many of the soldiers there live on our streets, their children attend our schools and they belong to our clubs and societies. They are a part of our town.

It was a major accolade to be invited to present campaign medals to some of the soldiers returning from Afghanistan. This was something I held in great esteem but also something I was nervous about; nervous about the fanfare, the scrutiny, the gravity, but mostly, I was scared that I was going to muck it up like the scruffy eight year-old boy I was.

The thing is, you can't just give someone their medal, you have to do a bit of chit-chat first. I was worried about going down the line dishing up sophisticated repartee to the soldiers. I should be able to do it but I was feeling the pressure. What would we talk about?

The burden got so much that I was prowling round the flat like a caged meerkat.

"What's up?" Hank asked with concern.

"Do you want the good news or the bad news?"

"Good news."

"Due to budgetary constraints the good news has been cancelled."

"Bad news?"

"I'm bricking it."

"You'll be fine."

"But what am I going to talk to all the soldiers about?"

"That's easy, just ask them what they do. They're all in the army, they're bound to do interesting stuff."

"You know…" I said, ruminating, "…that might actually work."

"Sorted, let's celebrate," Hank said, reaching for a bottle.

"Hank, I'm nervous. It's not so much that I have cold feet, its more that my trainers have frozen."

"What now?"

"Come on Hank, it's a big deal, these people have just spent six months in a war zone. I want to do it right. I'm on edge."

"Don't worry, I know just the thing to calm you down," Hank said, reaching for a bottle.

I had the cork out and the wine in the glass before I'd even thought about what I was doing. As I took that first harsh sip, as my body adjusted to the sharpness of the wine, I considered what had just happened. It seemed like Hank had control of my hands, as if he could instruct my body to do his bidding. Really? That was just silly.

Panic.

Eyes open.

It's light.

I'm late.

Body flooded with adrenaline. Mind reeled to catch up. I was groggy after last night's indulgences and

I had a vague memory of an alarm, an unformed idea about getting up early to prep.

Oh heck! I did not want to stuff this up. I did not want to look like I was a fraud who was out of his depth. I did not want everyone to think they'd made a mistake in appointing me.

I had to get a grip. I was tired because I had spent too much time pretending that the storm brought me calm. Maybe I could just hide? Properly hide, get a haircut and pretend my name was Algernon. I could do that, couldn't I? Well, no. I was just about the most recognisable person in the town. The local newspaper had started to resemble my photo album.

I was screwed.

Yet there was a glimmer. I was late, but not that late. Until the event starts there's hope. I had to act fast. Throw down a coffee. Pitch into the shower. Fling on a suit. Breakfast? A fool's paradise. Grab stuff. Late? It'll be tight but if you're breathing it's worth fighting.

I walked through the doors of the council offices – instant nerves. There were a lot of important people about. It didn't matter what people said about me, I could not believe that I belonged in this company. I was convinced that someone was about to tap me on the shoulder and say,

"Excuse me sir but you seem to be at the wrong event. This is the event for people who are successful, the event for frauds and fakers is down the corridor on the right."

Thankfully the only person showing me any interest was an affable young officer who was so tightly pressed he'd pass for dashing. I bet he hadn't slept through his alarm.

"Can I get you a coffee, sir?" he asked.

"That would be fantastic," I said with a gratitude that I hope wasn't too needy.

"I'll be your liaison for today, sir."

"Brilliant, can you show me to my dressing room?"

His initial confusion was promptly replaced with a grin that said we'd get on.

"Very good, sir. Shall I get that coffee?"

"Fantastic, and please call me Duncan."

"Thank you sir, but I have to call you sir."

"Really?"

"Yes there's a lot of high-ranking officers here today, if they hear me call you by your name I'll be tied to a pillion and lashed a dozen times."

"Really?"

"No, that's barbaric and would only happen in the navy. I'd just be offered what's known as an interview without coffee."

"That sounds worse."

As he disappeared to ferret out some strong black coffee I relaxed a little. Was it Sun Tzu who said 'having one ally in the world is to rock the big stage'?

I looked around the event to see who else was here. The council's elite were on show along with the Queen's representative in the county, diverse bigwigs, high-ranking officers and even some guy with a sword and a silly hat calling himself a high sheriff. He looked high to me.

"There you are sir," said the captain, handing me a cup of Java's finest.

"Thanks."

"I think the briefing is about to begin. I'm Captain Kermode, by the way."

We filed into one of the committee rooms; I found a seat at the back of the room but it offered little camouflage. A general strode to the front. He sported a combination of beady eyes and a hooked nose. I imagined that his hobbies included eating broken glass and sacrificing goats by moonlight.

He delivered his briefing with the kind of stern authority that is not intended to relax. It worked. Which was useful as I was still a little sleepy.

As we began to file out of the room the general approached me.

"Are you ready for this?" he said, his eyes blazing over his beak.

"I think so."

"You look," he paused, "a bit…"

Somehow I managed to hold his stone black eyes as he searched for the right word.

"...new to the role."

"Don't sweat it, I've got this," I said with a fabricated impudence.

There was something about that general that made me feel like a schoolboy again. I dismissed the thought. It was probably something that generals try to do. Most likely it's part of the job description.

As I strode out to inspect the troops, the wind brushed back my hair in what I assume was a very dramatic and macho way. The nerves started to abate – after all, I had a plan for this bit. I knew what to do, I knew what to say. They're all soldiers, they'll all have interesting jobs. I started to smile. I had this.

"Hi." It was not much of a gambit and it seemed to confuse the first soldier. I don't think his training had taught him how to answer such a casual opener. I ploughed on.

"What do you do?"

"Sir, I'm a driver."

We had a conversation about his truck. It was big. I congratulated him and gave him his medal. I moved onto the next soldier.

"What do you do?"

"Sir, I'm a driver."

OK. It turned out that he drove the same kind of truck. Congratulations. Medal. Move on.

"What do you do?"

"Sir, I'm a driver."

"You're all drivers aren't you?"

"This is a transport squadron, sir."

I was going to have a word with Hank when this was over.

To be fair to them, the soldiers helped me out. They were a great bunch – they passed me down the line bantering about football, girlfriends and the relative fizziness of the leading brands of premium lager. I was nearly at the end of the line.

"Sir, I'm not a driver."

"Fantastic, what do you do?"

"Sir, I'm a co-driver."

And that is why the British Army is the best in the world.

Immediately after the presentation I ducked into the loos. I needed a moment to landscape my psychic vista.

I looked into the mirror; I could see a faint scrub of black below my eyes, a faint grey pallour to my face and a faint stain of red across my lips, the evidence of last night's wine. I was only going to have one glass but somehow it had turned into two, then three, then Hank knows how many.

I thought about the soldiers I'd just met: the way they presented themselves, the way they sweat effort. I thought I was working hard, but these guys had spent months fighting supplies through some of the most dangerous parts of the world.

Even if I was averaging an event a day, working full time and cleaning enough to convince a new girl-friend that I was a reasonable human being, I *did not* have a hard life. Comparatively, my life was stress-free. Everything I did should have filled me with joy. I loved going to events. I loved making people smile. I was beginning to love Sreeja. My life should not have felt like a burden. Yet it did.

My contemplation was disturbed by Captain Kermode. Had he come to use the loo for its intended purpose or was this espionage? He gave nothing away.

"Is everything alright, sir?"

"For a moment there I was all at sea."

"Might I suggest another coffee, sir?"

"Might I suggest something stronger?"

He quickly checked the coast was clear.

"Well, Duncan," he said with a grin, "I think I can arrange that."

Sometimes one brother in arms is all you need.

Good to his word Captain Kermode came through with a rather pleasant glass of wine. The delicious drink and the enlivening conversation started something. But it had only raised a beast it could not put down again. The post-parade drinks were never going to be enough – it was time to move this party on.

I begged the good captain to come to the pub but apparently getting drunk in his parade uniform would lead him to the courts martial. So I made a call and in no time at all I was sitting in a bar with Steve, reliable Steve.

"That's such an honour," Steve said with an edge of frustration.

"What? You mean giving out campaign medals? Yes, I am pretty awesome am I not?" I said with just a touch of arrogance.

We lapsed into silence as we tended to our drinks.

"You know Billy Two Fists is having a party at the weekend?" He asked.

"Did I mention that I gave out some medals today?"

"You might have dropped it into the conversation."

"Yeah? I rocked it!"

I shut up long enough to take a couple of sips which must have been a blessed relief to Steve's battered ears.

"So are you free on Saturday night?" said Steve.

"Nope, wearing the chain, drinking the champagne."

"Oh sorry, I forgot that you are mayor of god damn everywhere."

I looked him in the eye with as much focus as I could muster. I couldn't have upset him, could I?

"Off the bar stool," he said with an undertone of menace.

"Why?" I asked nervously.

"You need to remember who you are."

Was he about to ask me to step outside?

"You need to remember where you're from and what's important and the only way to do that is to get off that bar stool and…"

He leaned in, ominous.

"Put your feet back on the ground." He broke into his trademark grin. "And taking your head out of your arse wouldn't go amiss."

Probably a fair shout and certainly preferable to a punch up.

I settled into the settee, but not before I'd opened a bottle and poured a glass: pints for the pub, wine for the win. I eased back into the chair. I felt like I'd been moving supplies across Helmand province when in fact I'd only been moving glasses across a bar.

"What a day." I said with a sigh.

"You did well," Hank replied.

"Did I?"

"Yeah, you rocked the show."

I looked at the council papers that littered my dining table.

"Did I?"

"Yeah, you're an awesome mayor."

I glanced over at the pile of washing up.

"Really?"

"It's difficult, you are under a lot of pressure."

The floor was a state. I really needed to Hoover.

"Right," I said with confidence and dynamism, "I'm going to sort this mess out."

I picked up the snakey, tubey bit of the hoover and tried to force it into the long, handley bit. For some reason, they wouldn't connect. It was like trying to reconcile science and religion.

"Come on, have a glass of wine before you break something," said Hank kindly.

"Look at the soldiers," I said pointing to an imaginary parade, "They're so buttoned up. If they don't have their stuff together they die. They are so in control. Why can't I be like that?"

"Have a little drink, it'll cheer you up."

"I have got to sort this place out," I said weakly.

"You deserve a drink."

I crumpled into the chair.

"You've had a hard day."

I took a significant gulp.

I tried to refill my glass, nearly knocking it over in the process. I realised that the bottle was coming to an end. A tidal-flow of fear pushed through me; it eddied its way into a lagoon of unease. My biggest logistics problem was to ensure there was enough wine for the evening, hardly Operation Overlord. It seemed that I wasn't even able to do that.

I couldn't manage life. I couldn't keep my flat clean. I couldn't get out of bed on time. When it came to anything as complex as being a mayor, I was aeons away from what was required. I was boasting in the pub even when I was mucking it all up. What a fraud. I couldn't get myself out the door in time, let alone do a decent job of the event itself. I wasn't just the Mayor of Failureton, I was piling up debts at the Bank of Acceptable Human Behaviour.

The wine's soporific effect was starting to drown me. I knew I should go to bed but I didn't have the energy, the motivation, the ability to stand. I bobbed on the wine-dark sea of my mind, one wave away from drowning.

I was lost. It was dark. I was stumbling. My senses were veiled in the night.

I sought light like a drowning man seeks air. The ground was choppy with roots. Every one trying to drag me down, down, down. On I swam.

A clearing. A fire. Safety. I sank onto a log. Calm, until I notice a brooding presence across the fire. A shadowy figure, his face hidden by a cowl.

"Allen?" I ask.

Somehow I could tell it was him, despite the fact that his face was obscured. Also, I had never met Allen – in fact he'd died before I even knew who he was. But something broke through the hole in my soul and told me that it was him, maybe it's because he was such a peerless writer that to read him is to know him, maybe it's because here the rules no longer applied.

He looked at me across the fire. I wasn't sure why he was wearing a brown robe. It was an unlikely ensemble for a man who was once a part time accountant and a full-time smoker but he looked reassuringly old Ben Kenobi.

"What are you doing here, Duncan?" he asked kindly.

"Staring at a fire is more interesting than watching TV?" I suggested.

"In that case, what am I doing here?"

"I don't know."

"Why was I here last time?"

"I needed to stop smoking."

For years I had struggled with cigarettes. Putting them down, picking them up, existing between the twilight and the darkness. Allen's book, The Easy Way to Stop Smoking, had changed all that. It made stopping smoking easy, which should have been obvious from the title. I thought about the joy that it had brought me, the many benefits that the freedom from smoking had given me.

"Maybe I'm drinking too much?" I said.

"Do you remember what we discussed when you stopped smoking?" he asked.

"We didn't discuss anything, I read a book."

"I think you should probably just run with this."

"OK, we discussed that the problem I had with smoking was believing that it gave me pleasure."

"Indeed."

"So what you're saying is, I should ask myself if alcohol is giving me pleasure?"

"Indeed."

"Well that's easy, I enjoy drinking."

"You do?"

"Think about all those great evenings of Bacchanalian excess – they were fantastic. Well, the bits I remember were. Obviously, I paid for it in the morning – what goes up must come down. But it was worth it, wasn't it?"

His penetrating look made me question whether I believed that.

"What about the evenings out with the lads? The larking and joking, that was fun wasn't it?"

"A lively evening with friends in a relaxed yet vibrant atmosphere – sounds great. What does it have to do with alcohol?"

I opened my mouth to reply but nothing came out.

"What *are* you doing here Duncan?"

Why was I here? I had a distorted picture of falling asleep feeling like a turkey at the end of November. I *must* enjoy drinking; that was why I did it so much, right?

"What does alcohol do for you?" Allen asked, stern but kind.

"Stress relief?" I said.

"And earlier, after everything you drank, did it reduce your stress?"

"I thought it did. It appeared to help me to relax."

"So it helped you have a calm relaxing evening?"

"Well no, I got thinking about the problems I've been having and they all seemed to get bigger. And if I'm honest, I might have been a tad obnoxious."

I paused as I began to hear what I was actually saying.

"I didn't have less stress at the end of the evening, did I?"

"If alcohol helped you cope with stress there'd be no stress in your life."

"Now you come to mention it, if alcohol got rid of stress – the amount I drink I'd be Buddha."

A cloud slid away from the moon, enlightening Allen's smile.

"I don't enjoy it, do I?" I admitted.

"Does anyone *really* enjoy it? From the moment we're born we've been brainwashed into believing that alcohol brings us comfort," he said.

"So what can I do?"

"Keep asking yourself the question, what does it do for you?"

"Absolutely nothing."

Allen smiled. The fire flickered. I thought, and thought, and thought.

It was a sports hall. They'd tried: they'd embellished the walls with balloons and banners, they'd filled the floor with people and in turn filled them with food and drink – but still it was a sports hall.

"Can I have a photo please Mr Mayor?."

"No worries," I replied for the thousandth time.

The event was celebrating the 50th anniversary of the independence of Nigeria. Why I'd been invited was a conundrum. Why I went was easier – it sounded intriguing and, besides, I'd go to the opening of a shopping bag – particularly if the bag had a bottle of wine in it.

The guy snapped half a dozen shots, then asked if his daughter could join me. "Sure thing." We arranged ourselves and he clicked off a few more photos. My smile wasn't just wearing thin, my face was starting to hurt. I have a highly developed view of how photogenic I am but even so, how could so many people want my photo?

"Please could we get a quick shot of you, Mr Mayor?"

"No worries," I replied for the thousand and first time.

I'm not saying the job was one-dimensional, but it was at times like these I wished I had a life size, cardboard cut-out.

I'd been through the door for 37 seconds and I had already kicked off shoes, thrown suit at hanger and hidden chain under bed. I decanted myself onto the couch. Another day at the mayoral coalface.

"You look knackered. Why don't you have a drink, dude?" Hank said.

"Hank, you're always there for me." I smiled and instantly regretted it.

"Grab a glass, man."

"I don't know Hank, I'm not sure I enjoy it any more."

"What do you mean? We always have fun when we have a drink."

"Have you ever thought that maybe it doesn't help us handle stress? It actually creates more stress?"

"Don't be silly. Sit down and have a drink."

"I don't know."

"You deserve it."

My resolve waivered for exactly the amount of time it took to take the corkscrew from the drawer, plunge it into the neck of the bottle and release the cork with a satisfying report.

How easy it is that we forget. Just a day ago I was sure that my life was not so tough, but now I thought I had it hard because I had to smile all evening. How easily we forget.

Have you ever noticed how the smallest people try to occupy the grandest rooms? It came as no surprise that Councillor Goodwillie had requested the most sumptuous room he could for our meeting. I didn't know why I was meeting him. Well, I imagined I knew what he wanted but why him? I would put money on the fact that we'd be discussing last weekend but who died and made him arbiter of standards?

What a farce Sunday had been. Saturday night had been a huge event that put me under a great deal of pressure. I had to deliver the keynote address and schmooze half the town afterwards. Of course I had drunk sparingly at that event but when I got home I was wound up like a clockwork traffic warden. Hank and I had opened a bottle or two to help me calm down while we watched Police, Camera, Action.

Then, in their infinite wisdom, the council had organised another event for Sunday morning. I use the word organise in the loosest possible sense. I'd done most of the real work – all they had done was put obstacles in my way. It was a shambles from start to finish. So I'd felt justified having a glass or two at lunch. Which, incidentally, was something I never normally did.

Now Councillor Goodwillie wanted a chat. He was one of the new batch of councillors but he paraded around with a fanfare that would have looked excessive on Louis XIV. That wasn't it though – it was the black holes he claimed as eyes and the crescent he passed off as a nose. They took me straight back to my schooldays, and that's what really bothered me.

By the time I had reached the council chamber a small quantity of smoke was coming out of my nostrils.

"You seemed a little unsteady at the lunch last week." Councillor Goodwillie said before I was through the door.

"I wasn't at my best, it's true. I was feeling a bit below par, that's all," I said.

"You looked – how shall we put it – strongly moved," he said with a grin.

"I was just tired."

"Really?"

My inner dragon was starting to stir.

"I have a very stressful life. It's hard being mayor and I didn't sleep well the night before. What do you expect me to do? Frankly the whole event was a shambles. You're lucky I only had a glass of wine, you're lucky I didn't start banging lines of coke off the table."

Councillor Goodwillie did not like this. Sod him. I was doing a great job. If I needed a little wine to help me through the stress, that was understandable. I didn't need to listen to this no-mark egotist telling me what I should and shouldn't do.

"It was a mistake to elect you. You don't have the dignity for the job. There is no way you can be the mayor you want to be."

Nowhere you can be? Time to bring the flames.

"Can you do anything about it?" I challenged.

He stumbled for a response and wordlessly acknowledged that he couldn't.

"Thought not. See you at the next civic knees-up."

I turned without waiting for his reaction. He was not worth my attention. I had char-grilled bigger chickens than him just to toss into a salad.

Out *here*
in the PERIMETER
there are no **stars**.

Jim MoRrison

A bathroom is a stupid place for your life to
change. It should happen somewhere more auspicious
like a court, a church or round the back of the bike
sheds. But as I glanced at Sreeja's face in the mirror, a
fusion of distrust and disbelief, things changed.

"Is that blue?"

"It looks blue."

"It is blue?"

"It is blue!"

Hugs, smiles, joy. I could have kissed the sky. I
was going to be a dad. Even though I was still a politician I had taken the extraordinary decision to spend
more time with the family and we had been trying to
enlarge it. We'd always said we'd wanted children and

now it was going to happen. There was delight, and, understandably, nerves too.

"What are we going to call it?" I asked.

"There are more important things to think about," she replied.

"Such as?"

"Will it be healthy, will it be happy, will it…"

"Like obscure Swiss folk music?"

"Duncan!"

"I think we should call it Twinkle."

Sreeja shot me a very eloquent look.

"A little Twinkle in their father's eye."

We hugged and agreed to drop the matter. But she wasn't wrong, there were more important things and one of them thrummed at the back of my mind: what about drinking?

How was I going to combine the late-night drinking with Hank that I enjoyed so much and the early morning demands that babies made? What if the baby woke up in the night and needed something like a bottle, a nappy or an in-depth critique of the Myth of Sisyphus? What would I do if I was, well, a bit pissed? And babies cost a lot of money – would there be any cash left over to buy cheap wine and expensive cheese?

I consoled myself with the thought that many of my friends who had children gave the distinct impression that, so long as the kids were in bed, drinking was completely acceptable. Hell, you could even buy baby-grows with "It's wine o'clock" on them, so I put it to the back of my mind. I'd think of something. Or Hank would.

Anyway, this was a happy time. A time to celebrate. What would we drink? Champagne? A superior red? Whatever it was we'd have to drink lots of it. Oh wait, Sreeja wasn't supposed to drink now. Should I wait till she went to bed? No, she'd understand and I'd get her some elderflower or something. Bottoms up.

A white sheet of A4, slightly curled at the edges, printed in a friendly font, advertising a gardening club. I don't know why I read it seven times; maybe it was because no one was talking. I stared at the gardening club advert and Sreeja stared at her hands, folded in her lap.

It felt like we had been sucked into an orbit, as if the health service was Saturn and all the patients swirled round it, arranged into various rings of varying size and splendor. We had been slotted into our rotation.

In this ring was the local midwife. Her large bosom seemed to guarantee the quality of her advice. She assured us that this appointment was nothing big, a natter and some encouragement.

Then she pulled from her drawer a strange device.

"I used to have one of those when I was a kid," I said enthusiastically.

The midwife gave me an odd look. She started to prod my wife's belly with the device.

"Funny thing to do with a walkie talkie?"

"It's a heartbeat monitor."

"Ohh."

The midwife ignored me and probed. She adjusted the angle and tried again. She looked at the monitor, hesitated and tried again. She tried again. And again.

"Is everything OK?" Sreeja asked like she knew it wasn't.

The midwife looked at the monitor, "They aren't the most effective things. They don't always work," she said with faux embarrassment.

I was perfectly willing to accept this but I could see Sreeja wasn't convinced. In fact, I suspected she was becoming apprehensive. The midwife could see this too.

"It's probably nothing."

Smile.

"Don't worry yourself but why don't you pop up to the big hospital to get it checked out?

Smile.

"Just in case." She hurriedly made us an appointment.

I looked at Sreeja. She was scared.

The table was large enough to accommodate half the council and was currently occupied by seventy percent of it. Meetings were not normally this well attended.

I'm not saying they're dull but their normal excitement level is somewhere between the static and the shipping forecast.

In fact, the big committee room was so full I had to stand at the back. The record attendance was because an evil corporation was threatening to dump fly-ash at a local beauty spot and the council was formulating its response.

I was excited. I flew at the meeting. I gave my opinion but I also listened and tried to bring the different sides to an understanding. I was engrossed in the verbal melee when Hank tapped me on the shoulder.

"Dude, it's nine o'clock," he said.

"Yeah, I know," I whispered back, hoping we weren't disturbing things.

"The shop round the corner closes at ten."

"Yeah, I know."

"We've got to buy two bottles of cheap French wine before it does."

"Yeah, I know."

"I'm just saying, this meeting appears to be dragging on a bit."

"Hank, shut up."

It's not that I stopped caring, I didn't. It was an assault on the environment – this was my reusable bag. A more focused person would have seen it to its end, would have pushed the point all the way. Me? I spent the rest of the meeting lamenting the impending closure of the shop round the corner. I zoned out. The end of the meeting couldn't come fast enough.

Same low ceiling, same rough-hewn walls; the place still felt like a cave. Kath still insisted on coming to this pub even though I no longer worked here. Of course I had called into the shop round the corner on the way – I wouldn't want to get caught short.

I had nearly finished my pint before Kath had sat down.

"A breakneck beverage? I trust this is not the dawn of the over-gratification of hard liquor?" Kath asked with a smile.

My eyes narrowed suspiciously.

"Are you enjoying that too much?

"No, I was just thirsty," I said off-hand.

"I knew another hep cat that used to sink his frothing ales that quickly and he drank himself into an awkward predicament."

I smiled. "Are you saying that I'm an alcoholic?"

"I wasn't saying…"

Really? I had her on the back foot already? I knew I could handle this line of enquiry without breaking an intellectual sweat but I wasn't expecting it to be this easy. It's as if all you need to do is say the word alcoholic and they leave you alone.

"Think about it – alcoholics pour vodka on their cereal, they can't hold down jobs and they get so drunk that when they drive home they can't remember where they parked their car. I've never done any of that so I clearly don't have a problem."

"It's merely that you sank your refreshment in some haste."

"What I have is technically known as a hankering. A little hankering for a glass of wine or two every now and again, maybe every day, and possibly some cheese. But I definitely don't have a problem. No issue, no trouble, just a little hankering."

I knew she wanted to respond but my logic was so watertight that she was stumped. I finished my pint.

"And what I have a hankering for now is another pint."

I strode to the bar leaving her to dwell on her intellectual spanking.

They tried to soften the edges but it was still a utilitarian tower block of medicine. Upon entering we were whisked to floor six and deposited in a beige waiting area.

The seating was comfortable but at the back of my mind there was a shadow. Was the baby OK? It had been easy to keep this thought on the fringes. It probably was nothing – after all, how good could one of those plastic machines be?

"What about Emmelzemus?" I said.

"You have got to be joking. That's not a real name." Sreeja replied with finality.

"All names had to be made up at some point."

I got The Look.

"I was on a website last night," she said, trying to rescue the conversation, "and it said that the baby will now be the size of an orange."

"That's great, I love vodka and orange."

"It's lucky I find you vaguely amusing."

"It would have been a long marriage if you didn't."

"No, it would have been a short one."

"Mrs Bhaskaran Brown?" interrupted a nurse. Her uniform was so crease-free that it looked like she'd got into nursing as an outlet for her OCD. I felt a jolt of nerves. But it was nothing to worry about, right?

Nothing increases apprehension and doubt like a darkened room – that and the forced air that hung about the nurses' work. She placed Sreeja onto the bed with a stiff wave. She squirted ultrasound gel onto her belly like it was clinical ketchup. I could feel the fear coming on.

She started scanning with a practiced disinterest. The unease took hold of my stomach, she swept the probe across Sreeja's abdomen. The consternation engulfed my heart, she pushed the probe harder. The dread overwhelmed my throat, she stared at the screen.

By the time the panic hit my brain it was over. There was no longer doubt. I knew. There was no heartbeat because there was no baby. There was to be no joy today, no joy any more.

She turned the screen away and rearranged her face into a concerned look. She sort of explained what had happened, but hedged her bets and left it to the consultant to confirm. She didn't need to say anything. I already *knew*.

This waiting room was sterile, barren, like a bad joke.

"When the hell are they going to see us?"

Sreeja did not answer.

I felt like I was waiting at a police station. Like my flat had just been burgled, my stuff ransacked, my possessions stolen. Now I had to sit in this damn waiting room hanging around for the privilege of seeing some bored cop who would type up my statement for the sake of the statistics.

I knew that this was the wrong thing to feel, that any reasonable human being would be desperate to help his shattered wife. That a better person would feel sad, yes, but that they're main concern would be to support their loved one through the confusion, the loss, the violation of their body. That's what someone normal would feel.

But I am not a normal person. I only felt like I'd been robbed, like something had been taken from me. God, I needed something, something to throw myself into, somewhere to expend my energy, somewhere to pour my adulation, my endless love. I needed this child.

I had been robbed. As hard as I'd try I'd never get over that. I'd always feel cheated, betrayed, like a promise had been broken.

"God damn it, where is the consultant?"

I had to get back to Hank. I yearned for wine. I craved the numbing darkness of oblivion. I needed the storm.

I was in prison. A cell packed full of angry, tattooed men who had sworn allegiance to one of the most homicidal gangs in the world. Well, I wasn't, I was on the sofa. Ross Kemp's strong, shaven head was poked through the door of a cell, surrounded by members of the maniacal Numbers Gang. I felt right there with him, only safer.

It was all part of Hank's plan to take my mind off it. He soothed me with wine, mollified me with cheese, and tranquilised me with TV. He knew how to make it better. Maybe he didn't do anything to solve my problems but at that point I only cared about getting through this moment.

We executed Hank's plan with pace, poise and audacity. Then Sreeja returned from the leisure centre. She did not greet me and, even in my deadened state, I could tell something was wrong.

"You didn't do the washing up," she said icily.

"I've been busy," I said in defence.

"What? Drinking yourself into stupidity?"

"I've been researching."

"What?"

"Well… I was thinking about writing something…"

"Why do you bother? You never even have the guts to show what you write to anyone."

My mind ground in search of an answer.

"Admit it, you'd rather spend time with a glass of wine than you would with me. You'd rather have a bloody kebab than a conversation."

How was I supposed to respond to that? It didn't matter because she was already in the bedroom, already closing the door.

Screw her. She didn't know. Damn it, I was trying. I'd done so much to help her. Forget her if she couldn't see it. She was lucky to have a guy who did so much. Let her keep her veil of steel and her deluded take on reality.

I ran through my usual circuit of complaints, working myself up until I couldn't spend another moment in that flat. I filled myself so full of indignation that I nearly managed to obscure the real reason I was running away.

I was running for the reason I always ran. The reason I jumped into the abyss every night.

Fear.

"Come on Hank, we're leaving."

The night felt like a pint of Guinness, black, heavy and chilled. I roamed aimlessly until I arrived at the centre of a bridge. The water below me roiled darkly. Downriver I could just about make out a bend but I had no idea what was past that. I turned slowly. To the other side was darkness. There seemed to be no direction to go in; backwards was ink black, forwards twisted into the unknown.

I looked down at the parapet in front of me. The seemingly solid edifice was, in fact, slowly crumbling. I took a swig from the wine bottle. If I hadn't been so damn independent I could have a well-paid city job. I'd probably have a nice family, a dog and two parakeets by now. I could've played golf on the weekends. Why had I chosen this path?

I looked Hank straight in the eye.

"What am I doing with my life?"

He didn't answer.

How did I end up here? The past was like a worn-down inscription in an archaic language. The future was even more impenetrable, even more unknowable.

Again I challenged Hank.

"Will I ever be a father?"

He said nothing.

This time I looked at him and begged.

"Can't I just be normal?"

Silence.

If Hank didn't know then I'd ask the river.

"Why can't I live without shame, booze, junk food and fear?" I shouted at the darkness.

The frigid river flowed on, unconcerned. I was angry. I was furious with Sreeja because I couldn't help her, because I couldn't get through to her. Was it time we went our separate ways?

The thought stung me. I'm no quitter. I do not give up. I overflow with resolve. But just then I wasn't sure what to hunt down. Did I even want to be a father? I thought I did but was it really my desire? Was it just some debris the world had lodged in my head? Who should I be? What should I be? *Where can I be?*

As light as the drizzle on the breeze I heard that voice again.

"Nowhere you can be..."

I took another acrid gulp from the bottle and watched the seething water. How could I ever cross the river?

I got **debts** that no HONEST man can **pay**.

BRUCE SPRINGSTEEN

I SCRUBBED THE LAST CAKE OF DIRT FROM THE LAST pan. I noticed Sreeja disappearing out of the room. The dinner time conversation had hardly been sparkling so I wasn't disappointed; she was going to read and would likely be in the bedroom for the duration.

Without much fuss and without any discussion we rebounded back to normal. After all, the rut we'd been wearing out for years was the easiest place to walk. So we kept on trudging. Down that furrow we went with our eyes on the floor, ignoring the scenery, ignoring each other.

"'You've had a hard day. A little drink will cheer you up – you deserve it." said Hank. I declined onto an easy chair and began to channel-hop. It seemed that

Ross Kemp had met all the gangs in the world and Police, Camera, Action hadn't started yet.

We alighted on Channel 5. As luck would have it, it was showing something more cerebral than Celebrity Bomb Disposal. The programme we found was about the brain and it was fronted by a casually dressed academic who was exerting far too much energy trying to look relaxed.

He was explaining that there are two parts to everyone's brain. There's the lower, less evolved part, the bit that is all about urges. The bit that is only really interested in sex and booze and McDonalds.

Then there's the higher, more evolved bit, the bit that actually makes decisions. The bridge of the Starship Enterprise that directs the engine room, beams people up and superintends all the various bits that make it boldly go. The bit that is actually in charge.

I looked at Hank.

Hank looked at me.

"More wine?" he asked with a smile.

Suddenly there was a snap like an overpaid football player rupturing a ligament. In a flash it all came together.

"That's who you are!"

With a starburst of clarity I realised Hank was my urges. He was my impulses, my basest desires – my lower brain. He was the less evolved bit of my mind that craves junk to drink and rubbish to eat. He was that little voice inside my head that whispers through the stress, through the pain, through the despair – "drink the wine".

For the first time in my life I looked him straight in the eye.

"That's what you've been up to all of these years. Squatting in unrepentant savagery in the deep dark recesses of my skull."

"But I'm your friend."

"Maybe you are, but your advice stinks because it is nothing but lust. It's lechery that'd make the devil blush."

"Very Shakespearean."

"Thanks."

"And you figured that out all on your own?"

"Yes, I did."

"You're one clever guy."

"I guess I am."

"Why don't you have a drink to celebrate?"

"Don't mind if I do."

Pop.

I cursed as I cleaned my stovetop espresso maker. Why was it always dirty? Why did Sreeja never clean it when she did the washing up? Was it not something that you washed up? I mean, I used it every day, several times a day. Why would I not need it clean?

God, I needed a coffee. My mind wasn't up to speed. Another night on the sofa. I wasn't in trouble, I'd just forgotten to go to bed. Again.

Then I remembered. It struck me like a grand piano falling from the eight floor, comedy sound effects and all.

"I worked you out. I know who you are now. I went all Colombo on you and now the mystery is solved."

"That bit looks clean, you can stop scrubbing dude."

"Thanks."

Please tell me it wasn't just one of those drunken flashes? A burning moment that seemed so profound but had reduced to nothing more than ashes.

I couldn't let that happen. I needed to take control; for once I wanted to be in charge of my life.

And I *was* getting closer to it, or at least I thought I was. Then again, maybe closer to the mirage means you're further from the oasis. Last night seemed like progress but today it had become fuzzy, unfocused, I was reaching out to grasp the heat haze.

I opened the coffee jar. Damn it! I'd run out – that's all I needed. Maybe I should just give up. I was trying to screw my courage to the sticking-post but I'd run out of screws. Maybe I had some No More Nails?

I was scared. Real, consuming, black, merciless fear. I stared at the wall; how could I do this? How could I make a decision? How could I judge? How could I pick?

I had jumped out of planes, crawled through tiny gaps hundreds of meters below ground, performed in front of thousands of people, but nothing compares to the gut-wrenching fear of judging a colouring competition.

I held the hopes and dreams of 30 five-year-olds in my hands – *that* is pressure.

I walked down the line of pictures. They were good. The children had clearly taken care to produce their best work; they were neat, proficient. But that was all. They looked like the products of effort rather than imagination. There's nothing wrong with effort but I wanted star-quality colouring.

Then I saw it. Instead of trying to render the sun on the trees this one showed the trees on the sun. My kind of colouring.

"That one," I said with certainty.

"Really? Are you sure?" the teacher replied with more than a note of surprise.

"Yes, that is our winner."

Sure, it was a touch messy but this child had taken a different approach and I admired that. Probably another mayor would have picked another winner; probably another mayor would have selected the neatest. Not me. The rock 'n' roll rebels of the world have got to stick together. I knew deep down in my DNA there was a fire that just don't quit burning. The same fire burnt in this picture.

The teacher ushered an unkempt boy into my presence.

"This is Arnold, your favourite artist." She clearly would have selected another picture.

"Well done Arnold," I said while trying to establish eye contact.

Nothing.

"I really liked your picture, it's not like the ones the other children did."

Nothing.

"Always remember to be a pig. Don't give in and become a chicken just because everyone around you is clucking and pecking."

That got a reaction. Admittedly it was confusion, but it was a reaction.

"What I mean is that it's OK to be yourself, even if you feel different from all the other children. It's OK. You are special.

Smile.

"The world is a big place, you'll find somewhere you can be who you're meant to be."

By the time I had given him his certificate he was beaming. I had brought the joy. Mission accomplished.

The precinct was bustling. I tried to weave between people but there was just too much crowd. Why did I bother shopping on Saturday?

"Duncan! Duncan!"

I twisted around to see a face I hadn't seen in a while. Jenny, a cracking lass who always took the business of pleasure seriously. I glanced down and spotted the pushchair. That's why I hadn't seen her in the pub for a while.

"Hey there, how's it going?" I asked.

"It's good babe, you?" she replied.

I didn't get to answer because the pushchair started to scream and required more urgent attention that I warranted.

"Sorry." she offered with a nervous smile.

"No worries. We should have a drink," I said.

"I'd love to, believe me, but I am so busy. I barely have time to sleep."

"Come on, you must have an hour or two? We could party like the old days."

"My lounge looks like a bad day in Baghdad. There's vomit everywhere and I haven't slept in way too long."

"That sounds exactly like the parties we had in the old days."

Rocking the pushchair back and forth was not working so she started walking. Apparently this was the only way that the child could be silenced. That left me holding the baby but only in a metaphorical sense. She handed me a bundle of thoughts that were shaped like a child. If Jenny had found normal maybe I could increase my store of contentment.

The cafe had changed. I was struck how close cool could be to bleak. How quickly chilling out could turn into freezing up. It was filling up with shoppers who were firmly outside of the demographic of hip. Had they started to sell tea cakes?

Clunk.

The waitress dropped my cake onto the table with a dull thump, I didn't notice. My mind was a sandstorm of hopes and fears and neurology. I knew who Hank was. But who was I? Who did I want to be? What was I going to be?

It was surging around my mind so much that I didn't notice the cake or the shoppers filling the place. Remarkably, I didn't notice the gingham clad grandma that approached my table.

"Excuse me deary, do you mind if I sit down?" she asked.

"Err... sure," I said.

I returned to my reflection and she bisected her scone with an expert flick of the wrist.

"Excuse me deary, do you mind if I ask you a question?" she said.

"Sure," I replied, still not entirely in the conversation.

"Is everything alright? It's just you look like you have the weight of the world on your shoulders."

"I have a..." I thought, "...problem."

"What I've learnt, over the years, is that if you have a problem you do something about it. Either that solves your problem or it gives you another problem."

"Uh huh."

"Then you do something and either that solves your problem or it gives you another problem."

"Uh huh."

"Then you do something and..."

"Either that solves your problem or it gives you another problem?"

"Exactly."

Now she had all of my attention, I was focused.

"So what you're saying is it's a cycle?"

"Exactly."

"Well that explains a lot. I'm really good at cycling."

She returned to her scone, carefully loading on the cream before the jam, an order I expect she'd fight to defend. I returned to my thoughts.

That was exactly it: I had a bad day, I'd drink and then the next day I'd feel terrible so I'd have a bad day, so I'd drink, which would make me feel terrible and that would make the next day seriously bad. Drink, feel terrible, bad day. Drink, feel terrible, bad day. Round and round and round I'd go, cycling and cycling and cycling. That was why my life felt like a punishing mountain stage of the Tour de France.

I plodded back through the precinct, every footstep an effort. She was right, of course, I understood every word she had said, just like I understood the documentary. I got it on an intellectual level. I just wasn't feeling it.

It was like walking on a knife-sharp ridge. On one side was the life that Jenny had found. A life full of bright plastic debris, bodily fluids and immeasurable joy. On the other side? Hank.

Part of me wanted to climb the tallest shop and shout, scream out the pain in my soul. I never asked to live in this zoo. I never wanted to be a good citizen. I never agreed to play by your rules. Part of me wanted to give in to Hank, to the darkness, to drink and smoke and snort and eat until there was nothing left to hoover up.

Yet deep inside me there was a near silent voice. I could barely hear it but it was calling me. What was it saying? If Hank would shut up for a while, maybe I could listen, maybe I could hear.

Despite the shopping centre cacophony, despite the bustle, I was sure I could hear *something*. I stopped in the tidal flow of shoppers. I closed my eyes. I took a long, deep breath. I rooted my feet to the floor. In the middle of that liquiform insanity I became as immovable as a tree stump.

I shut my mind to everything but the still, small voice. A whisper as insubstantial as a curl of smoke.

"How is that going to help me become a father?"

I sat on the edge of an armchair in a futile bid to read but I only managed to mentally relive a conversation I'd had a thousand times before. The conversation I'd had almost every night of my adult life.

"Let's have a drink."

"I don't know Hank, I should do the washing up."

"Leave the washing up, you've had a hard day, you deserve a drink."

"Erm…"

…and before I knew it a bottle was open and a glass was in my hand.

That conversation had happened over and over and over again. But tonight was going to be different.

Hank was nothing if not punctual. Bang on half eight he strode through the door looking as smug as a used car salesman that had just hustled his grandmother. I returned his smile. I knew what to say but I waited. I was, if anything, over confident.

"Let's have a drink," he said predictably.

"But Hank, how's that going to help me become a father?" I asked

"I think you should have a drink."

"How will a drink help me become a father?"

"I think you should have a drink?" Doubt had crept into his voice.

"But how's it going to help me have a child?"

"We always have a drink."

"How will wine bring a baby into my life?"

"Just the one?"

"How's it going to help me become a dad?"

"One drink can't hurt?"

"I want to be a father, Hank."

He looked at me, his eyes full of fear and confusion.

"I think I need to lie down."

That was it. That was all it took. One question and he was gone. There was so little to him that one question, a question that erupted from my heart, made him disappear. All of my life I'd been doing what he told me, even though the way to get rid of him was on the tip of my tongue.

He tried again the next night but his heart wasn't in it.

After years and years of listening to Hank, one question and he had crumbled. Sure, he popped back up a few more times but I just asked him the same question: "how's that going to help me become a father?"

To be fair, it actually took two questions. I also needed Allen to ask me if I was enjoying drinking. Once I'd accepted that I wasn't, then all I needed was a way to handle Hank. I thought I never could but, just by recognising who he was and giving him a name, I had gone a long way to getting him out of my life. The question was the last piece of the puzzle.

And once Hank was handled other things started to fall into place. Work got easier because I wasn't tired all the time. Concentrating was easier because I didn't have to worry where my next drink was coming from.

What really shocked me was the amount of time I had. I never thought I spent much time drinking because I'd only do it once the work was done; I'd rarely drink before half eight.

After a couple of days of my new life I had so much more time I started to think about it. I worked out that drinking from eight thirty till midnight was three and a half hours a day; that was a shade over 24 hours a week. It was like I had a whole new day, including the bit that I was asleep. I called it Dryday.

And I used the time wisely. I spent more of it with Sreeja. Our relationship improved because I was much more present when I spent time with her. No longer was half my mind chatting with Hank. We even took up a new hobby, dancing. We put a lot of time into learning the mattress fandango. And it paid off.

The willow by the window rustled. The view was so peaceful it could have been painted by a Zen monk. You could have mistaken the place for a spa, except there was a curtain that you could pull around the bed. I was so glad we had chosen a midwife-led unit rather than the fortress medico.

Almost to the day, nine months after I stopped drinking, I was holding a showroom fresh, latest model baby with tiny, state of the art fingers.

"She's beautiful," I said.

"You've done so well," said Sreeja softly.

"I know," I smiled back at her, "I did most of the work. I mean, the traffic driving here was awful but did you hear me complain? When we got stuck at that broken traffic light a lesser man would have folded, but not me."

"That wasn't what I meant," she smiled.

It hadn't been a meander in the meadow but we had made it. Unbelievably, there were more problems than the traffic. Of course, we had been nervous – who wouldn't be after a miscarriage? I was by no means perfect but I had more time, more mental space, more emotional capacity to talk through what we both felt about it.

We called our daughter Leela. It showcases her Indian heritage with the added bonus that you can pronounce it. It means 'divine play' and one day I hope to teach her that the entire universe is inside her, but for the moment I only wanted to dwell on the play bit. It was high time we played. It was time to bring the joy.

Caught BENEATH the landslide.

NOEL GALLAGHER

YES, THE CEILING WAS STILL LOW. YES, THE WALLS WERE still undressed stone. Yes, it still felt like a hobgoblin grotto. But something was different. Oh yeah, I was different. Well, a little different. My desire to visit public houses hadn't diminished.

That might sound strange but I was totally convinced I'd never drink again. Even if Hank had shown up I'd have put him back in his box without really thinking about it. I was confident in myself so why should the pub hold any fear?

Kath definitely hadn't changed. She insisted on drinking in this dive. Was that sawdust on the floor?

"What libations shall we lay waste upon the altar of Dionysus in the name of ritual madness?" she said.

"Can I have an orange juice?" I asked a little smugly.

"With vodka?"

"No thanks, I stopped drinking a while back."

"I do not doubt your verisimilitude. It must have been quite an exertion."

"Not really."

"Come on Duncan, it's all white knuckles and iron will, I never thought that was your knapsack. It must have been excruciating."

"Seriously, it's just a matter of rewiring your brain."

"That sounds even harder!"

"It's just a fancy way of saying change the conversation with the voice in your head. It's easy, trust me."

"No, I don't believe you. Stopping drinking is hard."

"Well, I found it easy."

"You probably weren't a proper alcoholic then," she smiled as she turned to order the drinks.

I let it slide. It wasn't that long ago that we were sitting here and she was accusing me of having a problem. It wasn't that long ago that I was sitting here bullying her into accepting that I was alright. But today? Today I let it go. Today I really was different, today I was calm enough not to start a ruckus. I knew what had happened to me, it mattered not what Kath thought.

Disarray. The floor was strewn with plastic and fur – to be expected. Not a single item of cutlery was clean – no surprise there. The bin overflowed like an eruption of garbage – not unusual. It was ten-thirty at night. Leela was not in bed. Something was wrong.

It was the first time I'd been out so late since Leela had been born, and it might have been a bad idea. As patiently as I could, I gave Leela a bath, put on a nappy and a clean sleep suit, warmed some milk, lay her in her crib and read her a couple of stories. Eventually she settled and with a long lingering look I wished her sweet dreams.

I returned to the living room and fought a plastic lion off the easy chair.

"The guy in the flat below is causing problems again. He's out to make my life hell. He makes noise so Leela can't sleep," Sreeja said, frosty.

"OK."

"He knows how hard it is for new parents, he's doing it deliberately so I can't get any sleep either. He tried to keep her awake at nap time too. He's out to get me. He's as bad as my mother."

"Well, it's quiet now. Let's get some sleep."

I could not sleep, but not because of the noises from downstairs.

Something was wrong. My mind was staggering about like a teenager on a Saturday night. I didn't want to admit it but part of me knew that Sreeja was getting paranoid.

As long as I'd known Sreeja she'd wrestled with her mental health. We'd had many good times and for most of our time together she'd been well, but she'd also descended into psychosis on more than one occasion.

We had not been unaware of the risks of having a child. Postnatal mental health problems are all too common with 30% of women suffering from them. The risk is even higher in women who have existing mental health conditions.

The consultant suggested that Sreeja took medication during the third trimester. I understood why she didn't want to do that and I completely supported her decision. The consultant suggested she took something after the birth. We were both reluctant because we both wanted her to breastfeed and the medication would have interfered. We agreed to closely monitor the situation.

Of course once Leela was born she was the only thing we closely monitored. By the time I was lying in bed struggling to come to terms with what was going on I doubt I would have been able to closely monitor anything more complex than The Gruffalo.

Shirt. Jacket. Shirt. Sreeja was emptying the contents of my wardrobe through our front door.

"Stop it," I said, scrabbling to return my clothes to the flat.

"I don't like these clothes," she replied, throwing a pair of trousers.

"I think you might be getting ill again," I said as gently as I could manage.

"I'm fine."

"I think it might be time for you to start taking medication."

"I think you should start taking medication."

"Why on earth should I take medication?"

"You have a lot of problems, especially with your mother."

It was laughable, but it really wasn't funny.

I needed to escape. Not like when I was child and I escaped to a fantasy world of heroes, villains and endless seascapes. Not like with Hank when I craved the dark and called it light. Now I really needed to escape, really needed to leave.

Once upon a time that was easy – grab the wine, open the door. But now I had a six-month-old baby to think about.

It was not a Hollywood escape. I heated up some milk. Threw some nappies and wipes into a bag. Strapped the baby-sling to myself and carefully loaded Leela into it. I grabbed the bag, the bottle and a muslin cloth. I was ready for my prison break.

I made it to the stairs but Sreeja had other ideas. She'd changed not just her character but her aura – it was like approaching a denuded tree in the depths of a Siberian winter. She blocked my path.

"Come on, let me go. I *need* to feed Leela," I said.

"You're not taking her away," she replied, level and deathly cold.

"No, I'm going to my parents so we can get some peace and I can give her some milk."

"You're *not* going anywhere."

I moved my hand to Sreeja's shoulder to encourage her out of our way. There was no force in the gesture, I had a bottle of milk in my hand. Moreover, I had a baby strapped to my chest. But for some reason Sreeja took this as a gesture of extreme violence and faux-stumbled down four steps. She didn't lose her footing and stopped when she bumped against the wall where the stairs turned. It was a sorry attempt to look hard done by. She was clearly unhurt.

I shook my head and walked past her.

The bright room was normally a place of joy, but today, hunched on the sofa feeding Leela, I was crying. It seemed likely that we would be staying at my parents' house for some time. I couldn't see how we could live with Sreeja. I couldn't see how we could escape. I couldn't see where we could be.

As I was getting myself tangled up in blue the doorbell rang.

"Mr Bhaskaran Brown?" his manner would have suggested police officer even if his uniform hadn't. I was a little intimidated, not just by his size but by the array of containment instruments dangling from his belt. He wanted some help with his enquiries so I let him in.

It turned out that Sreeja had phoned 999 and told them that I had pushed her down the stairs. PC Kearns politely pointed out that they had to take reports of domestic violence very seriously, I agreed. I also explained that Sreeja was not well, that she had been displaying signs of paranoia for some time and was not taking her medication.

He listened very civilly and just as affably told me that that was precisely what I would have said if I was trying to cover something up – fair point. Then he arrested me.

Sreeja came over to collect Leela and I got a ride in a police car.

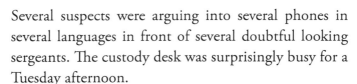

Several suspects were arguing into several phones in several languages in front of several doubtful looking sergeants. The custody desk was surprisingly busy for a Tuesday afternoon.

PC Kearns explained that he had to arrange an interview room. In the meantime he found me somewhere to wait. Frankly, the coffee I'd been given was bad. It was so bad it violated the Police and Criminal Evidence Act, the Geneva Convention and three separate human rights but I couldn't see a phone to order room service.

I sat down on the plastic mattress just pleased that it had been thoroughly wiped since the last inhabitant. I waited. I wondered. I worried. I waited some more.

I'd already planned our meals for the next two weeks so I was re-writing my mental shopping list when the service hatch snapped open, ensuring I would almost certainly forget to buy the oranges. PC Kearns peered through.

"There's been a development."

I was escorted out of the cell, down the corridor and into a room with one table, four chairs and a chunky tape recorder. It was just like on TV.

"My colleague was trying to take a statement from your wife and, while she was doing it, she became concerned about your daughter. Your wife wasn't making much sense," said PC Kearns.

"Uh huh." No development there.

"In fact, my colleague felt that your wife was so disoriented that it would be impossible to take a statement from her and that it would be unsafe to leave a child with her. My colleague got in touch with the mental health services and spoke with Sreeja's consultant. He was clear that Sreeja should have no contact with Leela from now on."

"Really?" *That* was a development.

"So we're going to release you so you can look after your daughter."

Two developments.

I considered pointing out that I was the one that had just been accused of domestic violence and I was the one that they thought was best placed to care for our child. I didn't as it would say more about the state of my life than their decision making.

Leela lay on a blanket gently gurgling to herself, happily oblivious to the maelstrom that was swirling around her. To avoid being sucked in I was clinging to a chair. Across the vortex was a business-like lady who was full of efficient compassion.

"This is a voluntary agreement but we're going to strongly suggest that Sreeja signs it," she said with gravity.

The official-looking paper weighed heavy in my hand.

"If your wife doesn't sign it, or agree to abide by it, then her consultant has indicated he may trigger the process of sectioning her."

It took me a moment to register what the woman from Children's Services had said. It was bad enough that we were apart but what would happen if Sreeja went to hospital?

"Surely that's a last resort?" I said.

"Yes, but you have to accept that your wife is close to checking into the last resort. If she doesn't start taking her medication, well…"

Her voice trailed off as if she thought I couldn't take what would follow. She was probably right.

"The last 24 hours has been the longest that Leela has spent apart from her mum. What are we talking about? Days? Weeks? Months?" I asked.

"What Leela needs at the moment is security. A calm, loving but above all stable environment. Sreeja can't provide that for her, but you can."

How had I got to this point? I still felt like that little kid who was hiding under blankets pretending to be an ocean-going sword of eco-vengeance. How was I supposed to be the sanctuary that Leela needed? I was barely a grown-up. How was I supposed to pick up the rock my life had become? I'm hardly Atlas.

God, I needed a knife. I grabbed one but I was instantly paralysed with doubt. Was I doing the right thing?

The question hammered in my skull: was this the knife that was used to cut pizza?

I hated my mother's kitchen. Yes, it was well appointed but there were standing orders and I had never read them – in fact, I hadn't even been issued with a copy. I always used the wrong knife.

Luckily Leela was fully occupying my mother, leaving me free to complete the onerous task of warming a pizza. I wasn't even doing a good job of that. What a mess. I looked at the pizza. I didn't want to, but it is important to look at what you are chopping, lest you cut off your fingers. I didn't want to look at it. I certainly didn't want to eat it.

For the last few weeks pizza had been my major food group and I was tired of it. Part of me was screaming out for home-cooked food. But if I could break so many rules warming a pizza then imagine how much trouble I'd get into if I actually tried to cook something. I gave in to the part of me that said I was too tired to cook.

I wondered what Sreeja was going to have for dinner. She'd been losing weight and I was sure she wasn't looking after herself properly. I wanted to do something but what? How could I look after her and Leela when I was struggling to look after myself?

Better make a start on the pizza.

I had given Leela a bath, dressed her, warmed her milk, read her some stories. As she was drifting off I started to run through my evening routine. It was exactly the same but I didn't have a bath, the milk was replaced with junk food and the stories with trash TV.

Leela stirred. I instinctively looked at her with that special panic reserved for parents who are convinced their children have stopped breathing when they clearly haven't. I thought about her future. What was going to happen to her?

"Nowhere you can be the child you're meant to be," I said softly.

If I was honest with myself, I was wondering what would become of me. Whether I could be the father I needed to be. Whether I could find some protection from the downpour. Nothing fancy; a bus shelter would do.

Mr Gannet flapped unbidden into my mind and for a second I was worried he might be right.

"Nowhere you can be..."

I plugged the headphones into my laptop and pressed play with as much conscious thought as I would give to breathing. I took a triple chocolate cookie from the packet with the same amount of consideration. My god they were sweet. I fumbled with the charger lead. As I reached for the next cookie, the sickness rising in my stomach suggested that one more cookie was not a good idea. I paused.

"Go on, you deserve it."

"I'm not sure, I don't feel great."

"Of course not, you've had a terrible day. All that stress you're under, you deserve it."

I picked up the cookie. In the darkness, Hank grinned.

London is DROWNIN', I, live by the **river**.

JOE STRUMMER & MICK JONES

I'M LOST IN THE SUPERMARKET.

Beep. Pizza. What the heck am I doing?

Beep. Cookies. I don't want any of this.

Beep. Muffins. An impending sense of doom.

Beep. Another pizza. Why can't I just get this mess under control?

I stared at the shopping as it moved down the conveyor. It looked like the ingredients for a kid's party where the main game was pin the sugar-crash on the child. Why was I buying all this junk, all this sweet, greasy rubbish? I didn't want it. I didn't need it. I didn't even like it.

I had to fight the urge to tear open the plastic packets and tear apart the plastic food.

"That'll be £25.36 please," said the checkout assistant breezily.

"What!" I almost screamed.

"£25.36," she replied with a look of fear on her face.

I banged my card onto the card reader.

I lugged my haul of salt, fat and sugar back to my parents, wondering why I can no longer shop happily.

It dawned on me that if I didn't have any sweet treats I'd get the same panicked feeling I used to get if I didn't have any wine. I realised that the way I was rushing to the shops to get junk food was the way I used to rush to get alcohol. It was hard to ignore, *I was eating like I used to drink.*

What was particularly stupid was that I knew how to get rid of Hank. After all, I'd done it before. But I didn't – I let him hang around. He prodded me to buy some cookies or some ice cream. He was always there to tell me that my arduous life meant I couldn't possibly cook, that I deserved a pizza for dinner. Most of all, he was there late at night when I tried to eat myself numb.

Sometimes you know exactly what to do, yet you don't do it.

The sucking gently slowed until Leela's cheeks became still. The teat slipped from her lips and I knew she was finally asleep.

I slumped back into bed. I had an early start but at least I could have another three hours of shut-eye. Well, maybe I could if I managed to distract myself from the slight ache in my stomach and the salt-induced dehydration.

And Hank.

What was I going to do with him? I was not the kind of person to dwell on such things. I was not the kind of person who worried about not being able to repeat their previous successes. I had got rid of Hank once before, I was not in any way worried about getting free from him again. That I could do.

But for how long? I was an all or nothing guy, a monster of habit. I was the kind of person who could get hooked on doing and undoing Velcro.

A question was thoroughly lodged in my mind: could I be free for good? Not just for a few months or even a few years but *forever*? There was an itchy fear that Hank would constantly be there, constantly waiting for me, constantly in the shadows.

I glanced at the bedside clock. Oh well, at least I could get two hours and fifty minutes of sleep.

Leela needed a baby walker. Strictly speaking she didn't need one; doubtless billions of babies had grown up perfectly happily without one. But I felt that she really ought to have one or society would think I was a bad parent – damn you society.

Leela was happily burbling away completely unaware of the circles of procurement hell that I was journeying through. And gosh, what an Amazonian rabbit hole I had fallen into. That one looked promising but it only had a three-star rating. What kind of parent buys their child a three-star baby walker? She'd like this one – it has a rabbit on it and she likes rabbits. If I bought that one could I join the Society of Awesome Fathers? Now *that* is a baby walker. That's the kind of baby walker that defines me as a person. Wait a minute, it's nearly three hundred pounds. Keep scrolling.

I looked over my phone for a second and took in the scrapheap of toys that littered the floor. I should tidy up.

Keep scrolling.

The day was cloudless. The air had enough chill to give it a bite but not freeze off any necessary anatomical parts. I breathed in the calm that emanates from trees that have seen much life drift past.

It was possible we might be turning Victorian. Leela and I had taken to promenading. Our daily turn around the park, while not necessarily the highlight of our day, was something worth getting dressed for and we seemed to both benefit from the fresh air.

We had grown inseparable from the sling that I carried her in. It was far more convenient than pushing round one of those high-performance baby barrows. But it also kept her closer to me. Sure, she could look out and see the world, but she could also snuggle in. It was, in essence, a way of making her hug me. And boy did I need the love.

"Duncan, Duncan!" It was Kath, my political mentor and bohemian thesaurus.

She looked at Leela poking out from her toasty pouch.

"Oh Duncan, her face could launch a thousand ships and burn the topless towers of Ilium. She's wondrous, she's perfect, she looks just like you."

"I hope not!"

"Don't be silly, she has your eyes. I'm sure she's going to grow up to be just like you."

"Here's hoping she doesn't inherit the beard."

The joke was stupid and pure instinct: Kath's comment shocked me. Was Leela going to be just like me? Was she destined to descend into drink? To drown in junk food? Was her life going to be dominated by Hank, just like her father's?

As I hurried back to the house I knew I had to do something. I had to be a better role model. I had to offer her a better example. I had to show her that there was another way.

I had to be a better parent.

Then an idea cudgeled me like a maltreated peasant. I had stopped drinking because I wanted to be a father. But that was the easy part. I was a father, I had a child, big deal. Now I had to *become* a parent. I couldn't say I was one just because I had a child. I had to live it every day. It had to infuse everything that I did. It's the difference between owning a tennis racket and winning Wimbledon, and I needed to work on my serve.

I pushed the trolley right, it tried to go left. I pushed it straight, it tried to go left. I stopped to grab some frozen peas, it tried to go left. It was like trying to collect smoke in a hessian bag.

I was staring at my shopping list. I had that nagging feeling that I'd forgotten something. Something that was just beyond the grasp of my consciousness.

"You forgot the ice cream, silly," chirped Hank.

"Oh, you think we need ice cream," I asked.

"We always need ice cream."

"How is ice cream going to make me a better parent?" I said it as casually as I could.

"You need it to relax."

"But how's it going to make me a better parent?"

"We always have a little treat?"

"How is it going to make me a better role-model for Leela?" I smiled. I was starting to enjoy this.

"Go on – I need it!"

"How is it going to help me become a better father? A better husband? A better human being?" I was on a roll.

Hank had nothing to say.

The supermarket may be an odd place to celebrate but at that moment I knew I was free. Free for good. I punched the air. And sod anyone who thinks it's weird to punch the air in the freezer section.

Even so, as my joy diminished I started to feel sorry for Hank. After all, it wasn't his fault. He was just playing the dead hand of evolution. Deep down he was trying to help me, he just got seduced by the quick wins of alcohol and junk food. I won't miss him but I bear him no ill will.

I pushed the trolley towards the checkout. I'm not certain but I swear the wheel was less wonky. It had started to push true.

Leela was lying on her back happily waving her hands at the camera. Sreeja was torn: part awash with love, part overcome with loss.

"She misses you," I said with as much compassion as I could find.

"I miss her," Sreeja replied.

"If you start taking your medication we can be a family again."

"The thing is..."

Sreeja never wanted to take medication, not paracetamol, not Lemsip and certainly not strong antipsychotics. I've never quite worked out why. Maybe it's because she doesn't trust authority figures, especially not doctors. Maybe it's because she has faith in her body. Maybe it's just because she's a big hearted, bloody-minded rebel. I don't know. But we always danced a few rounds of the 'take your medication' tango before she actually did.

How much more dancing would we need?

"Through this wide opening gate none come too early, none return too late."

After reading the inscription for the forty-second time I still hadn't figured out why they wrote it above the door to the council offices. It was starting to dawn on me that I might be putting off the inevitable. I had thoroughly examined the exterior of the building. It was assembled from Cotswold stone with industry and temperance – they don't make 'em like that any more. Maybe go through the door, Duncan?

The reason why I didn't want to venture inside was a certain Councillor Goodwillie. Even though I was no longer mayor I remained firmly on his hitlist. I reminded myself it was for a worthy cause. With all the courage I could muster I strode through the heavy wooden doors into the council offices.

"Your report is full of holes," Councillor Goodwillie said without looking up.

"Hello Councillor Goodwillie, how's your day going?" I said with a nailed-on grin

"Erm, OK," he looked flustered, "but we still can't support your proposal."

"They're a fantastic charity that's well run. They support young people who haven't had an easy start in life and, what's more, their work sits solidly within one of the council's strategic objectives."

"I disagree. We simply cannot support a charity that offers drugs and alcohol to young people."

"Where did you get that idea from?"

"From you," he said smugly, "It's in your report."

"Oh, I think you may have misread that. It says they offer drugs and alcohol *counselling* to young people."

"Nevertheless," he continued undeterred, "you also put in your report that they have unrestricted funding. If that's the case they don't need our help."

"Unrestricted funds is an accounting term that means that money can be used for any purpose. They don't have unlimited funding. They don't have a pot of gold, they're not leprechauns."

"Well, it hardly matters, I've already marshalled a lot of support to oppose this motion. You wouldn't want your reputation to be damaged by a costly defeat on the council floor." He eyed me from over his scimitar bill. "You could always withdraw the proposal if you want?" he said like a smiling, damned villain.

"No thanks, I'm good. If I've learnt one thing it is not to run away. See you at full council." That wiped the smirk clean off his face. I walked away as the balloon of pomposity began to deflate.

Beady eyed, hook-nosed bullies didn't scare me any more. Gone were the days I had to run away to feel safe. I no longer needed to escape to cope with life. In fact, the opposite was true. I needed to stand in front of life. I needed to straighten my back, clench my jaw and pretend that I knew what I was doing.

Very, very quietly I took down a knife. Very, very carefully I sliced a tomato. Very, very gently I placed the sandwich in a box. I was going to get away with this.

My mother burst through the door. Damn. Busted.

"Sreeja's looking really well," she said.

Excuse me? That was not a tirade. That was not a telling off. That was not what I had expected. She didn't even mention the knife.

"There's been such a change since she started taking her medication," she added.

"Like sunshine after a storm," I said.

"Your father and I were talking, we thought it was time you moved back into the flat."

"I don't know, it's still a bit delicate."

"Nonsense. She's much better and Leela would love to spend more time with her."

I hesitated, unsure. Yes, Sreeja was better but how long would that last? I didn't want us to return home only for it to crumble around our ears. The fear was still nibbling at my toes.

"And anyway, I want my kitchen back. Look, you're using the fruit knife to cut a tomato and that's the chopping board for bread and you're doing it all in the serving section. The preparation area is over there."

At least normal service had been resumed. At least some things could be depended upon. How normal would Leela's life be? How dependable were her parents?

Despite the myriad junk that littered the floor, Leela was crawling, and fast.

"Grab her," I said with urgency.

Sreeja scooped Leela up and they both giggled. We were all relishing being back together.

"Which is more humane: tying her legs to a chair or putting her under the washing basket?"

I got The Look.

"You spend ages hoping she'll learn to crawl and then as soon as she does you spend the rest of your time worrying about the dangers she'll crawl into," I said.

"I think it'll be like that until she's about twenty-five," Sreeja replied.

"Maybe all relationships are like that."

I'd spent so much time cajoling Sreeja into taking her medication and, now that she was, I was petrified about what would happen. As always, the change brought on by the medication was striking. Repairing the damage to our relationship would take longer.

When it was just the two of us Sreeja's illness had been hard on me. She would turn from a compassionate companion into a suspicious muckslinger. When she hurt me, I knew it was never her. I poured myself into a bottle and hid.

Leela on the other hand was different. What effect would it have on her? How long before she became aware enough to notice that it was all falling down around her ears? I don't claim to be the referee of Nature vs. Nurture but I figure poor mental health runs in families because it's so hard to live with a parent who's suffering.

We were crawling but what would we crawl into? The progress was so thin; just a handful of pills was the only substance. It was hard to start her taking them and I'd seen her stop at the drop of a stethoscope. I was nervous about her going backwards. Let's face it, I was worried about drifting myself. How stable was my recovery?

I was staring at a larger than life-size painting of a re-markably sane looking King George. For my money the artist had painted his head too small and his bum too big. It made no sense, George was the king, he could have had something done about that. But as far as I knew Gainsborough hadn't been beheaded so old George obviously liked the look. That really was mad.

The council chamber was awash with a post-meeting buzz. People chatted as they made their way out but even George's arse couldn't take my mind off my problem. Kath, that rococo force of nature, jolted me into the present as she took an elegant perch on the table in front of me.

"A monumental speech," she said.

"I don't know, I'm not feeling it," I replied.

"Look how the floor sparkles."

I looked but I couldn't see.

"It gleams because you just shined it with Councillor Goodwillie's face. You held a mirror up to him and showed everyone what a mutton-headed halfwit he is," Kath added.

"Making him look like an idiot is not hard. He usually does that on his own. I'm starting to think that I might be just like him."

"What? You're a great councillor and you've achieved a huge amount."

"Have I really had that much impact? Can I really do much from here?"

"There are a superabundance of people in this great land of ours but only one Prime Minster. Is the PM the only one that makes a difference?"

"No," I said, unsure where this was going.

"So don't worry about being PM, just try to be the best councillor you can."

"But I'm not sure I can be even a half-way decent councillor."

"Then just try to be the best human being you can."

I paused. Part of me just wanted to scream that there was nowhere I could be the person I needed to be. I had known that for years, it was obvious. Yet there was that hushed voice inside me that whispered, 'take one step closer to the person you want to be'.

"Be a bush if you can't be a tree?" I asked.

"That's about the measure of it," she said with a smile.

"If you can't be a highway, just be a trail. For it isn't by size that you win or fail."

"Hallelujah!"

"Be the best of whatever you are."

"Wow, that's deep. You're smarter than you thought."

"Actually, I'm better at remembering Martin Luther King quotes than you thought."

We both smiled.

"Just keep on improving and the rest will take care of itself," she said with a depth of compassion I'd never noticed in her before.

"Just keep improving." It rang round my head as we made our way out of the council chamber. Yes, I physically attended the post-meeting drinks but mentally I was obsessing over one question: how could I keep improving?

Leela would not stop crying.

I'd tried everything: much singing, many stories, a gallon of milk and my incomparable impression of an elephant eating a watermelon. Nothing worked. She just kept crying.

"Do *something*," Sreeja said with desperation.

"I've done *everything*," I replied tetchily.

"There must be something else?"

"Oh yes, let me just check '107 things to do when a baby called Leela won't stop crying', I'm sure it's on the bookshelf somewhere."

A baby that won't stop crying is bad. What the parents do to themselves is worse. Is she too hot? Is she too cold? Are the dangers of Calpol real? We're out of our depth. Should we call 111? Should we go to A and E? This is obviously our fault. Has she got meningitis? Chicken pox? Measles? Scrofula? We're clearly not fit to be parents. Call an ambulance. Call the army. Call God.

In all probability she was just teething but nothing prepares you for climbing that mountain other than climbing that mountain. It felt like I left my boots at base camp and I was holding my ice-axe the wrong way up.

Leela was asleep. Belatedly, quiet descended upon the flat. I glanced at the Stalingrad that our lounge had become and took the only decision that made sense. Sit now. Tidy tomorrow.

I squeezed onto the couch next to Sreeja and folded into the Rubik's hug we adopted whenever we watched TV. Except that neither of us reached for the remote. We just clung to each other in silence.

"Will we be OK?" Sreeja asked quietly.

"We love each other, we love little bear: everything else is detail," I replied.

"Yes, but there's been a lot of detail lately."

"I guess we just have to fight for it every day."

"Will every day be a struggle then?"

"Of course not, there will be good days along with the bad. What I mean is that we have to keep improving every day, even if it is only a little bit."

"That sounds like hard work. Can't we take tomorrow off?"

"Tomorrow yes," I laughed. "But, in general, if you're not moving forward today, you're slipping back to yesterday."

"I don't want to slip back."

"Me neither."

The hug tightened.

The path bent as it cut through the woods. The sun occasionally shot through the canopy. It was a little rocky but the gentle descent made it easy walking. It had a mystical calm like Led Zeppelin's more reflective songs.

The further into the woods we walked the more the tension faded. I was chilled out but Leela was so relaxed she'd fallen asleep in her sling. Even Sreeja was radiating a clam that I hadn't seen in a long time.

"I'm sorry," she said quietly.

"You are?"

"Yes, for what I put you and Leela through."

Maybe I should have told her that she had nothing to apologise for. Maybe I should have told her that I had already forgiven her. Maybe I should have told her that it was all just detail. I didn't.

"Thank you," was all I said.

We carried on walking.

I managed to haul myself off the sofa. It was well past my bedtime.

Putting Leela to bed was easy: bath, milk, stories. But my nighttime routine still hadn't settled. I was really going for it on the dietary front. I was no longer eating animal products. In fact, I had gone hell for vegan-leather-substitute towards a wholefood plant-based diet. Yet going to bed without alcohol or junk food still didn't quite make sense.

I brushed my teeth. It had been a normal sort of day: work, clean, play, hug. But then one thing had been absent.

Indulgence. There had been no alcohol for a couple of years and very little junk food for the last few months. It was a day without intemperance, a day that had been completely free of extravagance. Yet I didn't feel deprived.

I suddenly grasped the truth – for years I'd had it wrong. I thought if I wasn't overdoing it then I was depriving myself. In that moment it became clear. The opposite of indulgence is not lack or want, it's enough.

What I had accepted was that my job wasn't everything that I wanted – but it was enough. That the flat was not perfect – but it was enough. That my family had issues, and always would – but it was enough.

That was the easy part. When the bucket hit the bottom of the well, the struggle was accepting that I was enough. I wasn't everything I wanted to be, I wasn't perfect, I had issues and I always would but I *was* enough.

The *airwaves* were full of COMPASSION and **light**.

ROGER WATERS

THE SUN BLOSSOMED ONTO MY BED. I STRETCHED WITH rested ease as my eyes softly opened. I was at peace because I knew I wasn't late. I was tranquil because I slept well. That morning sparkled like dew in the early-bird sun. It felt like the start of the day was supposed to feel like.

I hope you know the feeling. I didn't know it for most of my life. Partly that was because Leela would wake me up in the middle of the night and I learnt why they use sleep deprivation as a form of torture.

Yet even before she was born I'd wake up tired. For a long time I just thought it was because I wasn't a morning person. I felt like I did my best work later in the day and hardly got started till after lunch. I'd heard all the theories about larks and owls and I'd decided that this was just the way it was – I stank in the morning.

Moreover, I didn't think there was anything I could do about it, I thought that was just who I was. I thought I had no more control over it than I did the colour of my eyes. It was written in my DNA the way Ursa Minor was written in the stars.

But now I understand that I felt bad on thousands of mornings not because of genetics but because of my lifestyle. Now all that was gone, this radiant morning felt like a second birth, like the start of a new life.

Planks of dark wood and little natural light; glowing spirit bottles and a stone floor that absorbs luminescence. It's almost as if they don't want you to realise it isn't nighttime. In fact, it isn't even lunchtime, yet we are in the pub. They'd hardly want to remind us that it might be a touch early for a drink.

"You want a coffee?" Steve said with indignation.

"Just a coffee," I smiled.

"Have a word! You've got to have a pint buddy."

"I haven't drunk for a couple of years."

A look of surprise crossed Steve's face. He begrudgingly sought out a coffee to go with his pint.

"What's all this about not drinking? Of all the people I thought you'd be the last one off the sauce," Steve said.

"I worked out how long I was planning to live, calculated the amount of units I was allowed over the course of my life and realised that I'd run out," I replied.

"Seriously, how did you do it?"

I sensed this was more than a casual inquiry. That there was a change but maybe Steve wasn't even aware of that himself.

"I guess it started when I asked myself if I was enjoying drinking," I said thoughtfully.

"But you love a drink, you're the life and soul," he said.

"What I was enjoying was the party, not the drink. I still enjoy spending time with people – it was never about the drink."

Steve thought while taking a pull on his pint.

"Isn't it a little bit about the drink?" he asked.

"I don't miss it. What I noticed was that the more I drank to relieve stress the more stress I had. So I asked myself, am I enjoying drinking? The answer was not a drop," I said.

Steve took a moment to consider this.

"Let's just say, theoretically, someone has decided that they aren't enjoying drinking. In this hypothetical situation, what would they do about it?" He asked as innocently as he could.

"I think it is important to realise that simply by asking the question you are doing something about it. Just accepting that it's time for a change is important."

"Yeah, but it's not enough is it?"

"But it is the first step."

"Happy days," his smile hid his impatience, "What's the second?"

"You have to realise that there is a part of your brain that has an urge to drink."

"I have one of those, possibly even two." He laughed.

"We all have them, we all have that little voice that tells us to drink, take drugs, smoke cigarettes, gamble, eat rubbish, buy rubbish, or stare at rubbish on our phones for hours on end."

"Even when you know you shouldn't?"

"Especially when you know you shouldn't!"

We both glanced at his pre-lunch drink.

"The voice that tells you to drink even when you don't want to. You need to give it a name. I call him Hank but it could be anything, male or female, human or beast. It doesn't matter what you call it, you just need to be clear who you are dealing with."

I could see this had Steve's mind racing. Actually, I could smell it.

"Mine's more of a Cassandra," he offered eventually.

"Whatever turns you on," I said, with a wry smile.

"Crack on then."

"Next you need a question to ask Cassandra. That way every time she suggests that you have a drink you know what you're going to say to her."

"What sort of question?"

"It could be as simple as 'how's that going to help?'"

"That I can remember."

"Or it could reflect what is most important to you. I asked Hank how a drink was going to make me a better parent because that was the most important thing to me at the time, but it might be about your relationships, your physical or mental health, your business, your job, money or self respect. Whatever matters most to you, right now."

"A name?" he considered this. "A question?"

We sat in silence for a moment as he absorbed it all.

"Just try it," I said. "You'll be surprised how little resistance Cassandra puts up. You'll get her under control quickly."

"Happy days. Then what?"

"Keep on keepin' on."

"Right on," he smiled and nodded, "what does that mean?"

"I think the biggest mistake people make is that they stop."

"But the point is to stop drinking."

"No, the point is to start. Don't stop drinking, start living. If you just stop drinking and don't do anything else, the rest of your life won't change. The reasons that made you want to drink will remain and at some point you'll let Cassandra sneak back into your life and you'll start drinking again or you'll just discover another destructive habit, like eating trash or staring at your phone for days on end."

"By start living you don't mean living on the edge?" he asked hopefully.

"No, it's time to step away from the edge," I replied, "you have to keep improving. Let's say drinking is your number one problem. You stop drinking. Do you stop having problems?"

"You'd have less problems."

"Yes, you'd have one less problem but all that means is that you'd have a new number one problem. So solve that."

"And when you've solved that you'd have a new number one problem?"

"Exactly."

Steve thought, looked at his beer and did not take a sip.

"Keep on keepin' on," he said, drawing out the words.

"I'm not saying that every day you have to make a massive change but you have to try to keep moving forward or you end up slipping back."

Steve's smile broadened into a full-on mischievous grin.

"So what did you improve today?" he asked.

"Ahh," I returned his grin, "at the moment I'm working on kindness. I've been driving on the M25 a lot."

"Tough place to be kind.

"When I see some poor driving, instead of shouting at the driver I try to forgive them."

"And that helps?"

"I think so. The more I forgive other people the easier I find it to forgive myself. I haven't hit outright enlightenment yet but I'm starting to forgive myself for some of the things that have been bothering me for years."

"Happy days."

We both smiled.

"You don't have to climb Everest every day, but every day you have to climb," I said.

"Let me recap for you," Steve said with a hint of showmanship. "Step one, ask yourself if you are enjoying it. Step two, give that little voice a name and ask them a question. Step three, keep solving the biggest problem you have."

"That's about it."

"It's good," he said with a laugh, "you should write a book."

As I opened the door I was assaulted with Knick-Knack Paddy-Whack blaring from the TV. The floor of the lounge was strewn with the kind of detritus only a toddler can conjure into existence.

"Daggy!" Leela shouted with the glee that comes with mastering a word for the first time. I was assailed with hugs. I realised there was nowhere else I wanted to be but here, in this exact moment.

I kissed Sreeja. Of late she had started to look well again, like herself, like the amazing woman I had fallen in love with.

As I removed my coat. Leela scampered up and pushed the remote control at me. Apparently, it was my turn to choose a song, and there was only one song that I wanted.

All You Need is Love rang out like the anthem of the nation of enough. I looked from Leela to her mother and reminded myself that I had enough, that all I needed was love. I busied myself with the mundane tasks of arrival, empty pockets, untie shoes.

"Nowhere you can be that isn't where you're meant to be," sang John Lennon.

What? Clearly, I'd never properly listened to this song before. Nowhere you can be that isn't where you're meant to be. I shivered like a goose had just walked across my grave. Then I grinned.

I was where I was meant to be. I had known that for some time but now there was more. I had never been anywhere that I wasn't meant to be. Yes, there had been a lot of pain and suffering, yes, I had done plenty of things I was not proud of, but I couldn't have got to where I was without being everywhere I had been.

Yes, at times my life felt like the shattered remains of Dresden after a visit from the Allied air force but I didn't have to regret the past, lament for what could have been or dwell on the wreckage. I had always been where I was meant to be.

And so have you.

The accumulation of everything that has ever happened to you has brought you to this point. It has helped you to accept that you want to remove overindulgence from your life.

You have taken the first crucial step. By picking up this book you've admitted to yourself that something is wrong. By finishing it you have accepted that you want to change.

You have recognised that you are no longer enjoying overindulgence. That it doesn't reduce your stress, it causes it. That it doesn't comfort you, it causes discomfort. That it doesn't relax you – in fact, it is the main reason you are so far from relaxed.

You have lived with your inner voice for many years, you know what it sounds like. It's time to give it a name so you can be completely clear about who you are dealing with. It's time to ask it a question so you can take control of the conversation.

You are capable of slow and steady improvement. You can improve your life a little every day for the rest of your life. You can keep solving your biggest problem. Like the man says, keep on keepin' on.

Everything that has ever happened to you has brought you to this point so you can act now, so that you can change your life. You can do it because *you* are enough.

BhaskaranBrown.com

Like to soundtrack?
Get the Spotify playlist here:
BhaskaranBrown.com/tunes

Speaker.

AUTHOR.

Morris **Dancer**.

While Duncan is obviously an author, and obscurely a morris dancer, he is primarily a big stage speaker. He is at his best in front of audiences numbering in the 1,000s or even in the 10s. He has spoken at conferences and events in the private and public sector, at universities, festivals and even the odd WI.

If you'd like to discuss him speaking at your event, then hit the keyboard and contact agent@bhaskaranbrown.com.

"I was glued to my screen from beginning to end."

ZANELE NJAPHA, EVENT ORGANISER.

"Incredible storyteller. True professional. OMG."

SIMONE VINCENZI, ENTREPRENEUR.

"Inspirational, practical, a dream to work with. Highly recommend."

LIZZIE BENTON, EVENT ORGANISER.

Acknowledgements

Without the kolaboration Deborah Henley and John Hayns this book would be simply a vague idea.

Big hugs for Leela and Sreeja, without them this book would be considerably shorter. A huge thanks to Oli Hudson, Andrew Fraser, Tom Ruder and Lorna Rooke for offering some constructive feedback. Praise and love to: Chantal Cornilius, whose advice is as good as her boots, Tanja Prokop and Graciela Aničić whose design work is beautiful and Martin Wackenier who actually enjoys taking crazy photos. Especial thanks to Robin Triggs whose sterling work makes me look literate.

Finally, big love for R and R, the best coffee-house Abingdon, without whom this book would be a good deal less caffeinated.

Printed in Great Britain
by Amazon

78547810R00084